ROYAL COURT

The Royal Court Theatre presents

IN THE REPUBLIC OF HAPPINESS

by **Martin Crimp**

IN THE REPUBLIC OF HAPPINESS was first performed at The Royal Court Jerwood Theatre
Downstairs, Sloane Square, on Thursday 6th December 2012.

IN THE REPUBLIC OF HAPPINESS

by Martin Crimp

Cast in order of appearance
Debbie/Teenage Girl 1 **Seline Hizli**
Mum/Middle-Aged Woman **Emma Fielding**
Hazel/Teenage Girl 2 **Ellie Kendrick**
Granny/Old Woman **Anna Calder-Marshall**
Grandad/Old Man **Peter Wight**
Dad/Middle-Aged Man **Stuart McQuarrie**
Uncle Bob/Man of About 30 **Paul Ready**
Madeleine/Woman of About 30 **Michelle Terry**

Director **Dominic Cooke**
Set Designer **Miriam Buether**
Costume Designer **Moritz Junge**
Lighting Designer **Peter Mumford**
Composer **Roald van Oosten**
Sound Designer **Paul Arditti**
Musical Director **James Fortune**
Casting Director **Amy Ball**
Assistant Director **Adele Thomas**
Assistant Designer **Lucy Sierra**
Production Managers **Paul Handley & Tariq Rifaat**
Stage Manager **Nafeesah Butt**
Deputy Stage Manager **Fran O'Donnell**
Assistant Stage Managers **Joni Carter & Sarah Hellicar**
Stage Manager Work Placement **Nikki Sammons**
Costume Supervisor **Jackie Orton**
Set built by **Miraculous Engineering**
Set painted by **Kerry Jarrett**

The Royal Court & Stage Management wish to thank the following for their help with this production:
Apple, Peter Jones, Jade Ward, Toby Williamson.

THE COMPANY

MARTIN CRIMP (Writer)

FOR THE ROYAL COURT: The City (2008), Rhinoceros (translation, 2007), Fewer Emergencies (2005), Advice to Iraqi Women (2003), Face to the Wall (2002), The Country (2000), Attempts on her Life (1997), The Chairs (translation, with Complicite, 1997), The Treatment (1993), No One Sees the Video (1991).

OTHER PLAYS INCLUDE: Play House (Orange Tree Theatre, 2012); Cruel and Tender (Young Vic/Vienna Festival, 2004); The Misanthrope (Young Vic, 1996); Getting Attention (West Yorkshire Playhouse, 1992); Play with Repeats, Dealing with Clair, Four Attempted Acts, Definitely the Bahamas (Orange Tree Theatre, 1984-9).

OTHER TRANSLATIONS INCLUDE: works by Botho Strauss, Genet, Marivaux, Koltès, Brecht & Chekhov for Sydney Theatre Company, the Almeida, RSC, National & the Young Vic.

OPERA INCLUDES: Into the Little Hill (Paris Opera, 2006); Written on Skin (Festival d'Aix en Provence, 2012), both with composer George Benjamin.

AWARDS INCLUDE: The 1993 John Whiting Award (The Treatment); Italy's 2005 Premio Ubu for the Fewer Emergencies triology.

PAUL ARDITTI (Sound Designer)

FOR THE ROYAL COURT, DESIGNS INCLUDE: Jumpy (& West End), In Basildon, The Pain & The Itch, A Girl In A Car With A Man, Duck, Plasticine, 4:48 Psychosis, Far Away, Blasted, Via Dolorosa, The Weir, Mojo, Shopping & Fucking, Some Voices, The Kitchen.

OTHER RECENT THEATRE & BALLET INCLUDES: The Magistrate, London Road, One Man Two Guv'nors, Blood & Gifts, Love the Sinner, Never So Good, Happy Now?, Saint Joan, The Revenger's Tragedy, The Year of Magical Thinking, Collaborators (National); Red Velvet (Tricycle); Three Sisters, The Changeling, The Beauty Queen of Leenane, Been So Long, Member of the Wedding, Vernon God Little, The Respectable Wedding, Generations (Young Vic); Company (Sheffield Crucible); Doctor Dee (ENO); The Most Incredible Thing (Sadler's Wells); Billy Elliot The Musical (West End, Broadway, Australia, US tour); A Ring, A Lamp, A Thing (Royal Opera House); Arabian Nights (RSC); The House of Bernarda Alba (National Theatre Of Scotland); When the Rain Stops Falling (Almeida); The Cherry Orchard & The Winter's Tale (The Bridge Project: New York, World Tour & Old Vic); Mary Stuart (Broadway); Under the Blue Sky (West End); Nakamitsu (Gate); Herge's Adventures of Tintin (Barbican & West End).

AWARDS INCLUDE: Tony & Olivier Awards for Best Sound Design (Billy Elliott The Musical); BroadwayWorld.com Fan's Choice Award (Billy Elliott The Musical); Olivier Award for Best Sound Design (Saint Joan); Drama Desk Awards for Outstanding Sound Design (Billy Elliott The Musical, The Pillowman); Evening Standard Award for Best Design (Festen).

MIRIAM BUETHER (Set Designer)

FOR THE ROYAL COURT: Love & Information, Get Santa!, Sucker Punch, Cock (& New York), Relocated, The Wonderful World of Dissocia (& EIF), My Child.

OTHER THEATRE INCLUDES: Chariots of Fire (Hampstead/West End); Decade (Headlong); Wild Swans, The Government Inspector, In the Red & Brown Water, The Good Soul Of Szechuan, Generations (Young Vic); Earthquakes in London (National); Judgement Day (Almeida); King Lear (New York); Six Characters In Search Of An Author (Chichester/West End/Sydney); The Bacchae, Realism (National Theatre of Scotland/EIF); The Bee (Young Vic/Japan); Guantanamo Honor Bound to Defend Freedom (Tricycle/West End/New York/San Francisco).

OPERA INCLUDES: Anna Nicole, Il Trittico – Suor Angelica (ROH); Carmen (Salzburg Festival);

Turandot (ENO); The Death of Klinghoffer (Edinburgh Festival/Scottish Opera); The Sacrifice (WNO).

AWARDS INCLUDE: Evening Standard Awards for Best Design (Earthquakes in London, Sucker Punch); Hospital Club Creative Award for Theatre 2008; Critics' Award for Theatre in Scotland for Best Design (The Wonderful World of Dissocia); The Linbury Prize for Stage Design 1999.

ANNA CALDER-MARSHALL (Granny/Old Woman)

FOR THE ROYAL COURT: Objections to Sex & Violence, Uncle Vanya.

OTHER THEATRE INCLUDES: Salt, Root & Roe (Trafalgar Studios); Danger: Memory: I Can't Remember Anything (Jermyn Street); The House of Bernarda Alba (Coventry); The Bargain, Troilus & Cressida (Theatre Royal, Bath); Love (Lyric Hammersmith); A Kind of Alaska, Tejas Verdes (Gate); Comfort Me with Apples, Formation Dancers, Dear Janet Rosenberg, While the Sun Shines (Hampstead); The Importance of Being Earnest (Oxford Playhouse); Birdcalls (Sheffield Crucible); Humble Boy (Gielgud); A Lie of the Mind (Donmar); Antigone (Old Vic); The Secret Rapture, The Devil is An Ass (National); The Philistines, Too Good to be True (RSC); Major Barbara, Twelfth Night, The Wild Duck (Lyceum); Absurd Person Singular (Criterion); The Country Wife (Prospect); The Lady's Not For Burning, Caesar & Cleopatra (Chichester Festival); St Joan, The Doctor's Dilemma, Peer Gynt, Measure for Measure/The Devil is an Ass (Birmingham Rep).

TELEVISION INCLUDES: Stage Door Johnnies, 13 Steps Down, New Tricks, The Bill, Poirot: After the Funeral, Holby Blue, Dalziel & Pascoe, Midsomer Murders, The Prince in Love, King Lear, Lovejoy, Heartbeat, Sherlock Holmes, Witness Against Hitler, Casualty, Strife, Inspector Morse, Titus Andronicus, The Winter's Tale, Androcles & The Lion, Strangers & Brothers, Days, Bloomers, Matilda's England, Under Western Eyes, Adelia, The Magistrate, Two Days in the Life of Michael Reagan, Arms & the Man, Somerset Maugham, Colombe, Male of the Species, Raging Moon, Girls in Uniform.

FILM INCLUDES: Anna Karenina, Zulu Dawn, Madame Curie.

AWARDS INCLUDE: Emmy Award for Outstanding Single Performance By An Actress (Male of the Species).

DOMINIC COOKE (Director)

FOR THE ROYAL COURT: Choir Boy, In Basildon, Chicken Soup with Barley, Clybourne Park (& West End), Aunt Dan & Lemon, The Fever, Seven Jewish Children, Wig Out!, Now or Later, War & Peace/Fear & Misery, Rhinoceros, The Pain & the Itch, Other People, Fireface, Spinning into Butter, Redundant, Fucking Games, Plasticine, The People Are Friendly, This is a Chair, Identical Twins.

OTHER THEATRE INCLUDES: Comedy of Errors (National); Arabian Nights, Pericles, The Winter's Tale, The Crucible, Postcards from America, As You Like It, Macbeth, Cymbeline, The Malcontent (RSC); By the Bog of Cats... (Wyndham's); The Eccentricities of a Nightingale (Gate, Dublin); Arabian Nights (Young Vic/UK & World Tours/New Victory Theatre, New York); The Weavers, Hunting Scenes from Lower Bavaria (Gate); The Bullet (Donmar); Afore Night Come, Entertaining Mr Sloane (Clwyd); The Importance of Being Earnest (Atlantic Theatre Festival, Canada); Caravan (National Theatre of Norway); My Mother Said I Never Should (Oxford Stage Company/Young Vic); Kiss of the Spider Woman (Bolton Octagon); Of Mice & Men (Nottingham Playhouse); Autogeddon (Assembly Rooms).

OPERA INCLUDES: The Magic Flute (WNO); I Capuleti e i Montecchi, La Bohème (Grange Park Opera).

AWARDS INCLUDE: Laurence Olivier Awards for Best Director & Best Revival (The Crucible); TMA/Equity Award for Best Show for Young People (Arabian Nights); Fringe First Award (Autogeddon).

Dominic was Associate Director of the Royal Court 1999-2002, Associate Director of RSC 2002-2006 & Assistant Director RSC 1992-1993.

Dominic is Artistic Director of the Royal Court.

EMMA FIELDING (Mum/Middle-Aged Woman)

FOR THE ROYAL COURT: Spinning into Butter.

OTHER THEATRE INCLUDES: Heartbreak House (Chichester Festival); The King's Speech, (Wyndham's/UK tour); Rock 'n' Roll (Duke of York's), Decade (Headlong); Playing With Fire, Look Back in Anger, Arcadia (National); Macbeth, Heartbreak House, 1953, School for Wives (Almeida); Cymbeline, Measure for Measure, The School for Scandal, Twelfth Night, A Midsummer Night's Dream (RSC); Private Lives (Albery/Broadway); Jane Eyre (Sheffield Crucible).

TELEVISION INCLUDES: Death in Paradise, The Suspicions of Mr Whicher, Kidnap & Ransom, The Cranford Chronicles, Fallen Angel, Ghost Squad, The Government Inspector, Beneath the Skin, Waking the Dead, My Uncle Silas, Green Eyed Monster, Inspector Lynley, Other People's Children, Big Bad World, Wings of Angels, Mrs Bradley Mysteries, A Respectable Trade, Dance to the Music of Time, Drovers' Gold, Kavanagh QC, The Maitlands, Tell Tale Hearts, Dread Poets' Society, Poirot, The Gist.

FILM INCLUDES: Fast Girls, 28K, The Great Ghost Rescue, Discovery of Heaven, Shooters, Pandaemonium.

AWARDS INCLUDE: The Dame Peggy Ashcroft Award for Best Actress (Twelfth Night, Broken Heart); The London Critics' Circle Theatre Award for Most Promising Newcomer (School for Wives, Arcadia); Ian Charleson Award (School for Wives); Carleton Hobbs Radio Award.

JAMES FORTUNE (Musical Director)

FOR THE ROYAL COURT: Posh (& West End).

OTHER THEATRE INCLUDES: A Midsummer Night's Dream (Filter/Lyric Hammersmith).

TELEVISION INCLUDES (as composer): Objects of Desire (Sky Arts).

SESSION WORK INCLUDES: Barry Adamson, Kate Nash, Sophie Ellis-Bextor, Tom Jones.

James is a songwriter and founding member/arranger for vocal harmony band The Magnets. The group has performed at The Roundhouse, London Palladium, Shepherd's Bush Empire, The Royal Albert Hall & the Edinburgh Festival Fringe, as well as on Parkinson, GMTV, & The BBC Proms in the Park. James' boxing song-cycle Journeyman: The Fall & Rise & Fall Again of Frankie Delaney will be produced in 2014 as part of Glasgow's Commonwealth Games celebrations. Lord of the Darts, the second show in his sporting trilogy, is currently in development.

SELINE HIZLI (Debbie/Teenage Girl 1)

FOR THE ROYAL COURT: Jumpy (& West End).

THEATRE INCLUDES: The House of Bernarda Alba (Almeida); One Night in November (Belgrade, Coventry); The Bacchae/Blood Wedding (Royal & Derngate).

TELEVISION INCLUDES: Appropriate Adult, Law & Order, Land Girls.

ELLIE KENDRICK (Hazel/Teenage Girl 2)

THEATRE INCLUDES: Romeo & Juliet (Globe).

TELEVISION INCLUDES: Game of Thrones, Being Human, Upstairs Downstairs, The Diary of Anne Frank, Lewis, Prime Suspect, Doctors, In2Minds, Waking the Dead.

FILM INCLUDES: Cheerful Weather for the Wedding, An Education.

RADIO INCLUDES: Dracula, Life & Fate, Plantagenet, Words & Music, The Resistance of Mrs Brown, The Shooting Party, Lady from the Sea.

MORITZ JUNGE (Costume Designer)

THEATRE INCLUDES: Damned by Despair, The Kitchen, Dido Queen of Carthage, The Hour We Knew Nothing of Each Other (National); Judgment Day (Almeida); All About My Mother (Old Vic); Blood Money (Theater Oberhausen); Cat on a Hot Tin Roof, Streetcar Named Desire (Theater Aachen).

DANCE INCLUDES: Undance (Sadler's Wells); L'Anatomie de la Sensation (Paris Opera Ballet); Live Fire Exercise, Limen, Chroma, Infra (Royal Ballet); F.A.R., Dyad 1909 (Wayne McGregor|Random Dance); Outlier (New York City Ballet); Dyad 1929 (Australian Ballet); Renature (Nederlands Dance Theater).

OPERA INCLUDES: Les Troyens, Aida, The Tempest (Royal Opera House); Messiah (English National Opera); Twice Through the Heart (Sadler's Wells); L'Elisir d'Amore (Theater Heidelberg); Don Giovanni (St Galle); Rigoletto (Staatsoper Hanover); La Cenerentola (Glyndebourne).

AWARDS INCLUDE: The Linbury Prize for Stage Design.

Moritz recently designed the costumes for the Opening Ceremony of the London 2012 Paralympic Games.

STUART MCQUARRIE (Dad/Middle-Aged Man)

FOR THE ROYAL COURT: Ding Dong the Wicked, Wanderlust, Relocated, Cleansed, Clybourne Park (West End).

THEATRE INCLUDES: Detroit, King James Bible Readings, Happy Now?, Scenes from the Big Picture, Ivanov (National); Marble (Abbey); Realism (National Theatre of Scotland/EIF); The God of Hell, The Dark, The Life of Stuff (Donmar); The Taming of the Shrew (RSC); Our Country's Good (Out of Joint/International tour); Shining Souls (Old Vic); The Government Inspector (Almeida); The Slab Boys Trilogy (Young Vic); Macbeth (Tron/Dundee Rep); The Thrie Estaites (EIF); Shining Souls, The House Among the Stars, The Life of Stuff, Hardie & Baird, Ines De Castro, Clocked Out, Loose Ends (Traverse); City Lights (PDB); A Midsummer Night's Dream (TAG); Laurel & Hardy, Good Morning Bill, Arsenic & Old Lace, The Bevellers, The Comedians, The Country Wife, Look Back in Anger, The Slab Boys, Mother Courage, Death of a Salesman, Charlie's Aunt, The Merchant of Venice, The Glass Menagerie, Hay Fever (Royal Lyceum); The Snow Queen (Dundee Rep).

TELEVISION INCLUDES: Blackout, Hustle, Lip Service, Any Human Heart, The Bill, Silent Witness, Extras Christmas Special, Whistleblowers, Peep Show, Taggart, Rebus, Black Book, A Very Social Secretary, Ghost Squad, Marian, Again, Golden Hour, Box of Slice, Life Begins, The Deal, The Way We Live Now, Four Fathers, The Echo, Butterfly Collectors, Silent Witness, Invasion Earth, London's Burning, The Peter Principle, Doctor Finlay, Taggart, Casualty, Hamish Macbeth, The High Life, Strathblair, City Lights, Ines de Castro, Loose Ends, The Justice Game, The Continental.

FILM INCLUDES: Blood, Closer to the Moon, Isle of Dogs, Burke & Hare, Another Year, House in Berlin, Franklyn, Hush, Young Adam, 28 Days Later, The Honeytrap, The Life of Stuff, Trainspotting, Love Me Tender.

PETER MUMFORD (Lighting Designer)

FOR THE ROYAL COURT: Jumpy (& West End), Our Private Life, Sucker Punch, Cock, The Seagull, Drunk Enough to Say I Love You?, Dying City (& set design).

OTHER THEATRE INCLUDES: Top Hat, Absent Friends, Much Ado About Nothing, The Lion in Winter, The Misanthrope, An Ideal Husband, Carousel, Fiddler on the Roof (West End); Betrayal (Crucible); The Last of the Duchess (Hampstead); Testament (Dublin Theatre Festival); A Streetcar Named Desire (Guthrie, Minneapolis); Heartbreak House (Chichester Festival); Pictures from an Exhibition (Young Vic); Parlour Song, Hedda Gabler, Cloud Nine (Almeida); Scenes from an Execution, All's Well That Ends Well, The Hothouse, Exiles (National).

OPERA & DANCE INCLUDES: (& concert staging/projection design) The Ring Cycle (Opera North); The Damnation of Faust, Lucrezia Borgia, Elegy for Young Lovers, Punch & Judy (Geneva); Bluebeard's Castle, Madam Butterfly (ENO); Faster, E=MC² (Birmingham Royal Ballet); Pelleas & Melisande (Mariinsky); The Soldier's Tale (Chicago Symphony); Madame Butterfly, Faust, Carmen, Peter Grimes, 125th Gala (New York Met); Eugene Onegin (LA Opera/ROH); Passion (Minnesota Opera); La Cenerentola (Glyndebourne); Carmen (& set design), Petrushka (Scottish Ballet); Il Trovatore (Paris); Fidelio, Two Widows, Don Giovanni, The Ring (Scottish Opera); The Midsummer Marriage (Chicago Lyric Opera); The Bartered Bride (ROH).

AWARDS INCLUDE: Olivier Awards for Outstanding Achievement in Dance (The Glass Blew In, Fearful Symmetries); Olivier Award for Best Lighting Design (The Bacchae); Knight of Illumination Award (Sucker Punch).

PAUL READY (Uncle Bob/Man of About 30)

FOR THE ROYAL COURT: Wastwater, Forty Winks, Terrorism, Black Milk, Crazyblackmuthafuckingself.

OTHER THEATRE INCLUDES: Noises Off (Old Vic/Novello); King James' Bible Readings, A Woman Killed with Kindness, London Assurance, Three More Sleepless Nights, Time & the Conways, Major Barbara, St Joan, Attempts on her Life, Mother Clapp's Molly House (with Aldwych), Waves (National); Love's Labours Lost (The Globe/US tour); The Pillowman (Curve, Leicester); One Flew Over the Cuckoo's Nest (Garrick/Nimax); Romance (Almeida); World Music (Donmar); Comedy of Errors (Bristol Old Vic); World Music (Sheffield Crucible); Romeo & Juliet (Liverpool Playhouse); Twelfth Night (Liverpool Everyman); Cuckoos (Gate/National Studio); Half a Bottle of Wine & a Kite (Crescent).

OPERA INCLUDES: The Beggar's Opera (Broomhall/Wilton's Music Hall).

TELEVISION INCLUDES: Utopia, Silk, Doc Martin, Pulling, Holby City, Trial & Retribution, Twisted Tales, Born & Bred, Blackpool, Life Begins, Jeffrey Archer – The Truth, Heartbeat, Tipping the Velvet, Chambers, Plain Jane.

FILM INCLUDES: Private Peaceful, Pierrepoint, Dresden, Maybe Baby, Angels & Insects.

RADIO INCLUDES: Twelfth Night, Romeo & Juliet, A Tale of Two Cities, Billiards at Nine Thirty, The Girl from the Sea.

ADELE THOMAS (Assistant Director)

AS ASSISTANT DIRECTOR FOR THE ROYAL COURT: Birthday.

OTHER THEATRE DIRECTION INCLUDES: The Passion, The Passion: One Year On (National Theatre Wales/WildWorks); The Bloody Ballad (Theatr Iolo); Dog Days for Write Here (Traverse); No Vacancies, Deluge (Sherman Cymru); A Doll's House, The Legend of the Golden Swans (RWCMD); Under Milk Wood (Royal & Derngate); A Cold Spread (Chapter); Big Hopes (NT Connections); Bulletproof (Replay); Repeat (Dirty Protest); Sennedd (Welsh National Opera); The Good Soul of Szechwan (Young Vic TPR); An Enemy for the People (Sgript Cymru).

AWARDS INCLUDE: Regional Theatre Young Director Bursary.

MICHELLE TERRY (Madeleine/Woman of About 30)

FOR THE ROYAL COURT: Tribes.

OTHER THEATRE INCLUDES: Comedy of Errors, London Assurance, All's Well That Ends Well, England People Very Nice (National); Sixty-Six Books – Fugitive Motel, 50 Ways to Leave Your Lover, The War on Terror (Bush); Light Shining in Buckinghamshire (Arcola); The Man Who Had All The Luck (Donmar); We the People, Love's Labours Lost (Globe); The Promise (New Wimbledon); The Winter's Tale, Pericles, The Crucible, Days of Significance (RSC); As You Like It (Newcastle-under-Lyme); Blithe Spirit (Theatre Royal, Bath/Savoy/tour).

TELEVISION INCLUDES: The Café (& writer), Reunited, Law & Order, Extras.

FILM INCLUDES: Runt.

ROALD VAN OOSTEN (Composer)

THEATRE INCLUDES: The Mahabharata (Frascati); Lollipop (Miek Uittenhout); Attempts On Her Life (Paul Koek).

FILM INCLUDES: The Van Waveren Tapes, Days of Grass, The Wild West.

AWARDS INCLUDE: Zilveren Harp Award.

Roald van Oosten writes & arranges songs. He released several albums with indie band Caesar including No Rest for the Lonely & Leaving Sparks, which was produced by Steve Albini, the recordist behind Nirvana. His most recent album release was The Grand Mystique with Ghost Trucker, with whom he performed at the prestigious Holland Festival.

PETER WIGHT (Grandad/Old Man)

FOR THE ROYAL COURT: In Basildon, The Seagull (& Broadway), Mouth to Mouth, Face to the Wall, Not a Game for Boys.

OTHER THEATRE INCLUDES: Otherwise Engaged (Criterion); Ivanov, Sleep With Me, Murmuring Judges, Arturo Ui, Black Snow, Waiting for Godot (National); The Spanish Tragedy, Much Ado About Nothing, Barbarians, A Clockwork Orange, Hamlet (RSC); The Caretaker (Globe Theatre, Warsaw); Edward II (Royal Exchange, Manchester); Dearly Beloved, Grace (Hampstead); A State of Affairs, Othello,

Comedia, Progress (Lyric Hammersmith); The Seagull (Lyric Hammersmith/UK tour); Chekhov's Women (Lyric West End); Julius Caesar (Riverside); A Passion in Six Days, A Midsummer Night's Dream, The Nest (Sheffield Crucible); King Lear, Three Sisters (Birmingham Rep); The Seagull (Shared Experience); Hard To Get (Traverse).

TELEVISION INCLUDES: The Paradise, Hit & Miss, Public Enemies, Titanic, Money, Monday Monday, Boy Meets Girl, 10 Days to War, Party Animals, Dalziel & Pascoe, EastEnders, Persuasion, Fantabulosa, Waking the Dead, Murder Prevention, Early Doors, Silent Witness, Murphy's Law, Uncle Adolf, Brides in the Bath, Charles II, 40 Something, Midsomer Murders, The Second Coming, Care, Active Defence, The Project, The Blind Date, The Passion, Our Mutual Friend, Jane Eyre, Wokenwell, Out of the Blue, Anna Lee, Hearts & Minds, Meat, Devil's Advocate, Speaking in Tongues, Codename Kyril, Exclusive Yarns, Save Your Kisses, Yesterday's Dream.

FILM INCLUDES: Another Year, Womb, Atonement, Hot Fuzz, Lassie, Babel, Pride & Prejudice, Vera Drake, The Statement, 3 Blind Mice, The Gathering, Lucky Break, The Fourth Angel, The Shiner, The Return of the Native, Personal Services, Fairy Tale, Meantime, Naked, Secrets & Lies.

THE ENGLISH STAGE COMPANY
AT THE ROYAL COURT THEATRE

'For me the theatre is really a religion or way of life. You must decide what you feel the world is about and what you want to say about it, so that everything in the theatre you work in is saying the same thing ... A theatre must have a recognisable attitude. It will have one, whether you like it or not.'

George Devine, first artistic director of the English Stage Company: notes for an unwritten book.

photo: Stephen Cummiskey

As Britain's leading national company dedicated to new work, the Royal Court Theatre produces new plays of the highest quality, working with writers from all backgrounds, and addressing the problems and possibilities of our time.

"The Royal Court has been at the centre of British cultural life for the past 50 years, an engine room for new writing and constantly transforming the theatrical culture." Stephen Daldry

Since its foundation in 1956, the Royal Court has presented premieres by almost every leading contemporary British playwright, from John Osborne's Look Back in Anger to Caryl Churchill's A Number and Tom Stoppard's Rock 'n' Roll. Just some of the other writers to have chosen the Royal Court to premiere their work include Edward Albee, John Arden, Richard Bean, Samuel Beckett, Edward Bond, Leo Butler, Jez Butterworth, Martin Crimp, Ariel Dorfman, Stella Feehily, Christopher Hampton, David Hare, Eugène Ionesco, Ann Jellicoe, Terry Johnson, Sarah Kane, David Mamet, Martin McDonagh, Conor McPherson, Joe Penhall, Lucy Prebble, Mark Ravenhill, Simon Stephens, Wole Soyinka, Polly Stenham, David Storey, Debbie Tucker Green, Arnold Wesker and Roy Williams.

"It is risky to miss a production there." Financial Times

In addition to its full-scale productions, the Royal Court also facilitates international work at a grass roots level, developing exchanges which bring young writers to Britain and sending British writers, actors and directors to work with artists around the world. The research and play development arm of the Royal Court Theatre, The Studio, finds the most exciting and diverse range of new voices in the UK. The Studio runs play-writing groups including the Young Writers Programme, Critical Mass for black, Asian and minority ethnic writers and the biennial Young Writers Festival. For further information, go to www.royalcourttheatre.com/playwriting/the-studio.

"Yes, the Royal Court is on a roll. Yes, Dominic Cooke has just the genius and kick that this venue needs... It's fist-bitingly exciting." Independent

Jerwood Theatre Downstairs

15 Feb – 9 Mar 2013

if you don't let us dream, we won't let you sleep

by Anders Lustgarten

A new play exploding the ethos of austerity and offering an alternative.
Part of the Royal Court's Jerwood New Playwrights programme, supported by the Jerwood Charitable Foundation.

21 Mar – 27 Apr 2013

the low road

by Bruce Norris

A fable of free market economics and cut-throat capitalism.

Jerwood Theatre Upstairs

Until 22 Dec 2012

hero by E.V. Crowe

A bracing new story of a heroic modern man.
Part of the Royal Court's Jerwood New Playwrights programme, supported by the Jerwood Charitable Foundation.

ROYAL COURT

11 Jan – 9 Feb 2013

no quarter

by Polly Stenham

An anarchic twist on the drawing room drama.

22 Feb – 23 Mar 2013

a time to reap

by Anna Wakulik translated by Catherine Grosvenor

An exciting new voice looking at Poland's hottest political topics – abortion and the Catholic Church.
International Playwrights: A Genesis Foundation Project.

5 Apr – 4 May 2013

a new play

written and directed by Anthony Neilson

Renowned for his ground-breaking new work, Anthony Neilson returns to the Royal Court.

17 – 26 Jan 2013

rough cuts

New work exploring our relationship to the internet.

The Studio is supported by The Andrew Lloyd Webber Foundation. *Rough Cuts* is supported by the Columbia Foundation Fund of the London Community Foundation.

Wilson Rehearsal Studio, Royal Court

Until 5 Jan

constellations by Nick Payne

An explosive new play about free will and friendship.

Royal Court Theatre Productions and Ambassadors Theatre Group

Duke of York's, St Martin's Lane, WC2N 4BG

25 Jan – 23 Feb

feast

a new play by **Yunior García Aguilera** (Cuba), **Rotimi Babatunde** (Nigeria), **Marcos Barbosa** (Brazil), **Tanya Barfield** (US), **Gbolahan Obisesan** (UK)

A Young Vic and Royal Court co-production

Young Vic Theatre, SE1 8LZ

020 7565 5000
www.royalcourttheatre.com
⊖ Sloane Square ⇌ Victoria 🅱 royalcourt 🅵 theroyalcourttheatre

Principal Sponsor **Coutts**

Supported using public funding by
ARTS COUNCIL ENGLAND

ROYAL COURT SUPPORTERS

The Royal Court has significant and longstanding relationships with many organisations and individuals who provide vital support. It is this support that makes possible its unique playwriting and audience development programmes.

Coutts is the Principal Sponsor of the Royal Court. The Genesis Foundation supports the Royal Court's work with International Playwrights. Theatre Local is sponsored by Bloomberg. The Jerwood Charitable Foundation supports new plays by playwrights through the Jerwood New Playwrights series. The Andrew Lloyd Webber Foundation supports the Royal Court's Studio, which aims to seek out, nurture and support emerging playwrights.

The Harold Pinter Playwright's Award is given annually by his widow, Lady Antonia Fraser, to support a new commission at the Royal Court.

Principal Sponsor

Supported by
ARTS COUNCIL ENGLAND

INDIVIDUAL MEMBERS

GROUND-BREAKERS

Anonymous
Moira Andreae
Allen Appen & Jane Wiest
Mr & Mrs Simon Andrews
Nick Archdale
Charlotte Asprey
Jane Attias
Brian Balfour-Oatts
Elizabeth & Adam Bandeen
Ray Barrell & Ursula van Almsick
Dr Kate Best
Stan & Val Bond
Kristina Borsy & Nick Turdean
Neil & Sarah Brener
Mrs Deborah Brett
Mrs Joanna Buckhenham
Louise Burton
Clive & Helena Butler
Sindy & Jonathan Caplan
Gavin & Lesley Casey
Sarah & Philippe Chappatte
Tim & Caroline Clark
Christine Collins
Carole & Neville Conrad
Anthony & Andrea Coombs
Clyde Cooper
Ian & Caroline Cormack
Mr & Mrs Cross
Andrew & Amanda Cryer
Alison Davies
Matthew Dean
Roger & Alison De Haan
Noel De Keyzer
Polly Devlin OBE
Glen Donovan
Denise & Randolph Dumas
Robyn Durie
Zeina Durra & Saadi Soudavar
Glenn & Phyllida Earle
The Edwin Fox Foundation
Mark & Sarah Evans

Margaret Exley CBE
Celeste & Peter Fenichel
John Garfield
Beverley Gee
Nick & Julie Gould
Lord & Lady Grabiner
Richard & Marcia Grand
Reade & Elizabeth Griffith
Don & Sue Guiney
Jill Hackel & Andrzej Zarzycki
Carol Hall
Jennifer & Stephen Harper
Sam & Caroline Haubold
Madeleine Hodgkin
Mr & Mrs Gordon Holmes
Damien Hyland
The David Hyman Charitable Trust
Amanda Ibbetson
Nicholas Jones
David Kaskel & Christopher Teano
Vincent & Amanda Keaveny
Peter & Maria Kellner
Nicola Kerr
Philip & Joan Kingsley
Mr & Mrs Pawel Kisielewski
Sarah & David Kowitz
Rosemary Leith
Larry & Peggy Levy
Imelda Liddiard
Daisy & Richard Littler
Kathryn Ludlow
Dr Ekaterina Malievskaia & George Goldsmith
Christopher Marek Rencki
Andy McIver
Barbara Minto
Shafin & Angelie Moledina
Ann & Gavin Neath CBE
Murray North
Clive & Annie Norton
Georgia Oetker
Mr & Mrs Sandy Orr

Mr & Mrs Guy Patterson
William Plapinger & Cassie Murray
Andrea & Hilary Ponti
Lauren Prakke
Annie & Preben Prebensen
Mrs Ivetta Rabinovich
Julie Ritter
Mark & Tricia Robinson
Paul & Gill Robinson
Sir & Lady Ruddock
William & Hilary Russell
Julie & Bill Ryan
Sally & Anthony Salz
Bhags Sharma
J Sheridan
The Michael & Melanie Sherwood Charitable Foundation
Tom Siebens & Mimi Parsons
Andy Simpkin
Anthony Simpson & Susan Boster
Paul & Rita Skinner
Mr & Mrs RAH Smart
Brian Smith
Mr Michael Spencer
Sue St Johns
The Ulrich Family
The Ury Trust
Amanda Vail
Constance Von Unruh
Ian & Victoria Watson & The Watson Foundation
Matthew & Sian Westerman
Anne-Marie Williams
Sir Robert & Lady Wilson
Daniel Winterfeldt & Jonathan Leonhart
Kate & Michael Yates

BOUNDARY-BREAKERS

Anonymous
Katie Bradford
David Harding
Steve Kingshott
Emma Marsh
Philippa Thorp
Mr & Mrs Nick Wheeler

MOVER-SHAKERS

Eric Abraham
Anonymous
Lloyd & Sarah Dorfman
Piers & Melanie Gibson
Lydia & Manfred Gorvy
Mr & Mrs Roderick Jack
Duncan Matthews QC
Miles Morland
Ian & Carol Sellars
Edgar & Judith Wallner

MAJOR DONORS

Rob & Siri Cope
Cas Donald
Jack & Linda Keenan
Deborah & Stephen Marquardt
NoraLee & Jon Sedmak
Jan & Michael Topham
Stuart & Hilary Williams Charitable Foundation

Thank you to all our Friends, Stage-Takers and Ice-Breakers for their generous support.

In the Republic of Happiness

Martin Crimp was born in 1956. His plays include *Definitely the Bahamas* (1987), *Dealing with Clair* (1988), *Play with Repeats* (1989), *No One Sees the Video* (1990), *Getting Attention* (1991), *The Treatment* (winner of the 1993 John Whiting Award), *Attempts on Her Life* (1997), *The Country* (2000), *Face to the Wall* (2002), *Cruel and Tender* (2004), *Fewer Emergencies* (2005), *The City* (2008) and *Play House* (2012). He has a longstanding relationship with London's Royal Court Theatre, and more recently with the Vienna Festival and the Festival d'Automne in Paris, which commissioned his first text for music, *Into the Little Hill* (2006), written for composer George Benjamin. His second collaboration with Benjamin, *Written on Skin*, premiered at the Festival d'Aix-en-Provence in 2012. He has also translated works by Ionesco, Koltès, Genet, Marivaux, Molière, Chekhov and Bruckner.

MARTIN CRIMP

In the Republic of Happiness

an entertainment in three parts

1 DESTRUCTION OF THE FAMILY

2 THE FIVE ESSENTIAL FREEDOMS
OF THE INDIVIDUAL

3 IN THE REPUBLIC OF HAPPINESS

First published in 2012
by Faber and Faber Limited
74–77 Great Russell Street, London WC1B 3DA

Typeset by Country Setting, Kingsdown, Kent CT14 8ES
Printed in England by by CPI Group (UK) Ltd, Croydon CR0 4YY

A CIP record for this book
is available from the British Library

ISBN 978-0-571-30177-5

2 4 6 8 10 9 7 5 3 1

Characters

Eight actors are required, as follows

PART ONE	PART TWO	PART THREE
Grandad	Old Man	
Granny	Old Woman	
Dad	Middle-Aged Man	
Mum	Middle-Aged Woman	
Debbie	Teenage Girl 1	
Hazel	Teenage Girl 2	
Madeleine	Woman *of about thirty*	Madeleine
Uncle Bob	Man *of about thirty*	Uncle Bob

Assignment of roles

In Parts One and Three
roles are assigned in the usual way.

In Part Two
there are no assigned parts,
and the whole company should participate.

A dash before a speech —
indicates change of speaker.

DESTRUCTION OF THE FAMILY

Daylight. Christmas.

A small artificial tree with lights.

The family is gathered: Mum, Dad, Granny, Grandad, Debbie, Hazel.

Dad stares at Debbie. Silence.

Debbie I wasn't trying to upset people, Dad. I love you. And I love Mum. Plus I love Granny and Grandad – and of course I love Hazel too. I do, Hazel – whatever you think. But the fact is, is I know that I'll love my baby more. And that's how it should be, Dad – however much I love you, I know that I'll love my baby more. Which is why I'm afraid. Wouldn't you be afraid? When you look at the world? – when you imagine the future? I'm afraid, Dad – for my baby. And I'm really sorry because I know this is Christmas and I shouldn't be talking like this about horrible things but it's just I can't help it.

Mum You mustn't apologise, Debs. Tommy's not really angry – are you, Tom.

Hazel So why doesn't she just get rid of it?

Mum Hazel doesn't mean that.

Hazel Yes I do – if the world isn't 'good enough'.

Granny That's not a nice thing to say, Hazel.

Mum She doesn't actually mean it.

Hazel Yes I do.

　　Pause.

9

Mum So you went to the supermarket, Margaret.

Granny Oh it's not very interesting.

Mum *We* think it's interesting. What did you get? Come on – tell us – cheer us all up.

Granny Well – I bought a lettuce –

Mum Really?

Granny Yes.

Mum A nice one?

Granny Yes quite a nice lettuce, and a packet of biscuits.

Mum Wonderful!

Granny Oh and some material for your Grandad.

Debbie Material? What kind of / material?

Hazel She means pornography. (*To Grandad.*) Why don't you just get it off the internet, Grandad?

Granny He's frightened someone will steal his identity, Hazel – and anyway it's always much nicer having the actual magazine.

Mum Well I'm very sorry but I think that's wrong. I wouldn't buy pornography for Tommy.

Debbie Please stop it, Mum – why 're you trying to make Grandad feel guilty? It's not as if he's going to *do* anything – he just likes looking – looking's not a crime.

Grandad Don't you talk about me like that, young lady. I am neither senile nor impotent – surprising as that may seem.

Debbie Sorry, Grandad – in fact I was defending you – but in future I'll keep my mouth shut. Okay?

    Pause.

Granny Where're all the light bulbs, Tom?

Mum What's wrong, Margaret?

Granny What's happened to all the light bulbs? There's none in the toilet and I'm just looking and it looks to me like there are none in here either.

Hazel It's because electricity's got so expensive, Granny.

Granny Well yes – I know electricity's expensive but eventually it will get dark. What happens when it gets too dark to see?

Hazel We get the box out of course.

Granny What box?

Mum The box with the light bulbs in – don't we, Tommy.

Pause.

Tommy? Is something the matter?

Dad D'you think this bird's been properly cooked?

Mum Why 're you asking me that?

Dad It's just that ever since we started this meal I've felt a bit sick.

Granny You can't 've done, Tom – of course it's cooked – it's delicious, Sandra.

Mum Thank you.

Granny Exceptionally succulent.

Mum Thank you.

Granny Which part did you stuff?

Mum The neck.

Granny Because you know not to stuff the body.

Mum Of course not: I stuffed the neck.

Granny Don't stuff the body – it won't cook.

Mum I didn't.

Granny You're sure? Because these bacteria can be very /
dangerous.

Mum I know what I've stuffed.

Granny Well anyway, I think it's excellent.

Mum Thank you.

Dad Then why does my mouth taste of vomit?

Granny It can't be the bird, Tom.

Dad Well in that case it must be my particularly selfish
daughter bringing up yet again the subject of her
unplanned and ill-conceived pregnancy in front of this
whole family when *she can't even name the father*.

Debbie I'm sorry, Dad.

Mum Don't bang on the table like that.

Dad I'll bang how the fuck I like.

  Pause.

Granny He's been like this ever since he was little.
People don't change. But he does need to control his
temper – especially at Christmas.

Dad Yes, Mum – okay – I take your point – I'm sorry.

Granny People don't change – you learn that when you
get to my age.

Hazel But you've changed, Granny.

Granny I don't think so. How?

Hazel You used to be young and pretty.

Mum Hazel.

Hazel Well it's true: people don't change is rubbish.

Granny And what did Santa bring you for Christmas, Debbie?

Debbie Well I can't honestly go asking for presents when I've already got the most marvellous gift of all.

Hazel Lying cow – I saw the list!

Debbie What list?

Hazel She made this long long list of all the things she wanted – and because she's pregnant she got them.

Mum Please. Hazel.

Hazel The hat – the radio – the car – the 'nice little diamond earrings'.

Debbie I need a car to get to the hospital for my scans – and anyway you got that dress.

Hazel Why doesn't she use the bus? Granny's old and she uses the bus. So what if I got a dress – big deal – it wasn't exactly expensive.

Dad Mum? – on a bus? – you're joking – when did you last get on a bus, Mum?

Mum Leave your poor mother alone, Tommy.

Granny No he's right – because in fact, Hazel, your father is right, I don't use the bus, I take taxis. I may be an ugly old granny – as you have so kindly pointed out – but I still like to sit in the back of a taxi and be driven through the streets – especially at dusk in summer with all the smells of plants and restaurants coming in through the window – and all the childless young people in light summer clothes swarming on the pavements outside the shops and bars. I like to watch the meter running. I like to think ah these two minutes in a taxi have already cost me what that man emptying the bins will take more than an hour of his life to earn – and oh the extra stink of a rubbish bin in summer! Yes on nights like that the taxi is glorious and the fact I'm paying for my happiness makes my happiness all the sweeter – and the fact that other people are having to suffer and work just to pay for such basic things as electricity makes it even sweeter still. And when I'm cruising the clogged streets watching all those people your age, Hazel, all those childless and carefree people swarming outside the bars like ants outside of an ant-hole, I sometimes wonder if we are not on the verge of some enormous and magnificent change – don't you think? Yes I mean a change to our actual human material. Compared to which your sister's pregnancy – unplanned and ill-conceived as it may well be, plus medicalised beyond all reason by those same profitable concerns who have so often flown me (oh I admit it) to conferences and booked me into comfy hotel rooms – compared to which reproduction of your sister's kind – involving some kind of man, some kind of penetration, and even perhaps (I'm just guessing now, Debbie) some kind of wide-eyed love – might only be capable of churning out more of the same – more and more of exactly the same – and is that what we really want? Because what I'm imagining – Hazel – in that taxi of mine, is a new kind of magnificent human being who may not even be human at all.

Hazel Well I still don't see why she needs a car.

Mum The thing is Hazel sweetheart is that's not for you to decide. And just because Debbie puts something on her list it doesn't mean she automatically gets it.

Hazel She got the car.

Mum She needs the car to go to the hospital.

Hazel And I suppose she needs those earrings to go to the hospital too.

Debbie storms out.

Mum Please don't leave the table – please – please don't storm off like that – she doesn't mean it.

Hazel Well I'm sorry but I think the way you're both spoiling her is horrible.

Pause.

Dad Very interesting, Mum – what you just said.

Granny Oh I know you think I'm an idiot, Tom.

Dad Not at all, not at all.

Mum Look I know I'm just your mother, Hazel. And I know that means I'll shop and cook and clean for you for ever and ever. You'll come home from your second failed marriage just like I'm sure you'll come home from your first just like you used to from school trips with a big bag full of dirty washing and expecting your dinner. And that's fine. If you can't make a marriage work, that won't be your fault. I agree that men with their fat thighs and their legs apart on trains can be impossible and that unselfish and faithful men like Daddy, or like Grandad here, are the exception, not the rule. Yes, I'm just your mother, and as such I expect to be trodden on and trodden on – I expect to be worn away like a stone step – and I'm prepared – like the stone – to endure it. But that doesn't mean I've no feelings, Hazel. My heart isn't stone too.

Hazel I'll go and talk to her.

Mum Thank you.

Hazel goes.

Are you alright there, Terry? Would you like some more meat?

Grandad Because I am neither senile, I'll have you know, nor impotent. – Just a little, please. – I won't be put down and I won't be put into a home. There are all kinds of erections – an erection doesn't have to be rock hard – it can still be useful. I never locked him in a cellar. I never abused you, Thomas – and I never abused your mother – not even when it was the fashionable thing. I've spent my whole life swimming against the tide. Well of course I had a mortgage, but I paid it off – nor do the police frighten me: I don't commit crimes – not serious ones – so don't think you can make me believe I'm losing my memory then shut me away in a home. I've paid my way – there's money in the bank and I'll spend it however I like: I happen to enjoy ice creams and speedboat rides – that doesn't mean I'm a child or can be treated like one. Remember you're looking at a man who spent forty years in general practice and ten years before that in prison for a crime I never committed – so when men went into space, is it surprising I envied them their weightlessness? I wanted Tom to go into space – I'd hold him up when he was little and show him the moon – remember that, Tom? – remember those teddy-bear pyjamas? He could've walked on the moon – he needn't have spent his whole life processing planning-applications – but he had no spark – the moon was too far – he couldn't be bothered.

Dad is looking at him.

What?

Dad You were never in prison, Dad. You were never a doctor.

Grandad I never said I was, Tommy boy. I'm not stupid.

Mum Let's not start an argument.

Dad Why not? He loves it.

Mum was the doctor, Dad. Mum worked for forty years to support you. The reason you have money in the bank now for speedboat rides and pornographic downloads is that while you squandered, Mum constantly worked.

Granny He helped me in the house, Tom.

Dad Helped in the house? He can't even load a washing machine.

Granny You've no right / to insult him.

Dad Whatever. He can't hear me anyway.

Grandad Of course I can hear you: you're the one who's deaf.

Dad I may be going deaf – yes – but at least I have the intelligence to wear my hearing aid and actually switch it on.

Mum You're being cruel now.

Dad Correct.

Grandad What?

Dad Oh for godsake . . .

Grandad *What* did he say?

Dad I said correct, Dad – I am deaf – correct – you're right – you're absolutely right – forgive me.

Oh hello, what's this?

Debbie and Hazel have reappeared as perfect friends.

Friends now, are we?

Debbie Yes, Dad. Sorry.

Hazel No: it was my fault. I'm really sorry, Mum. I've been a complete cunt.

Mum Well as long as you're friends now.

Granny What's going on, girls?

Debbie We're going to sing for you, Granny.

Mum Sing?

Hazel We want to sing for you all like we did when we were little.

Mum Well that's wonderful!

Dad Is it something we know?

Debbie It's something we both made up.

Debbie and Hazel sing.

Debbie / Hazel

> We're going to marry a man
> (going to marry a man)
> The man will be rich
> The man will say bitch:
> > I'll make him pay for my meals
> > I'll strut and fuck him in heels –
> That's our incredible plan
> Yes our incredible plan.
>
> We're going to carry a gun
> (going to carry a gun)
> The gun will go bang
> and puncture the man:
> > I'll aim my gun at his head
> > I'll pump his balls up with lead –
> Oh what incredible fun
> Yes what incredible fun.
>
> We're going to sharpen a knife
> (going to sharpen a knife)
> The knife will be real
> The blade will be steel:

> I'll cut my name in his thighs –
> cut out his tongue if he lies –
> That's how to be a good wife
> Yes how to be a good wife.
>
> We'll send our man to the moon
> (send our man to the moon)
> The moonlight will shine
> on your man and mine –
> > I'll keep his rocket on track
> > I'll make him radio back:
> *Oh darling marry me soon*
> (yes darling – marry me –
> oh marry me soon)

Enter from the background where he has silently appeared: Uncle Bob.
Uncle Bob wears distinctive clothes, perhaps a well-pressed polo shirt and brand-new jogging pants.
Uncle Bob claps.

Uncle Bob Marvellous – marvellous singing, girls.

Girls Uncle Bob! Uncle Bob!

Uncle Bob Girls! Hello! Sandra! Tommy! Margaret! Happy Christmas!

Girls Happy Christmas! Happy Christmas, Uncle Bob!

Some of the others also murmur 'Happy Christmas'.

Uncle Bob Marvellous – what a marvellous song.

Mum What're you doing here, Robert?

Uncle Bob Well to be frank with you, I've really no idea. I thought I would just suddenly appear, so I did. I suddenly appeared. I craved your company – craved to be with you all – and here I am. I hope I'm not putting you out at all.

Dad Of course not – you're very welcome.

Mum Girls – fetch Robert a chair.

Uncle Bob Oh no no no no no – no chair for me – I can't stay.

Granny You've only just arrived.

Uncle Bob I still can't stay.

Hazel Please – please stay – why can't you?

Debbie Please make him stay, Mum.

Uncle Bob Listen – I'd love to stay. You think I don't want to? Of course I want to. What a marvellous warm house, and what a great great welcome you've all given me. There are so many reasons to stay here – and all of them really persuasive: the smell of roast meat – red wine – the crackling log fire* – these two lovely girls with their whole lives ahead of them – and even – if my instincts are right – and they usually are – they usually always are – even – in beautiful young Debbie's case – yes look – the promise – and how appropriate to the time of year! – the radiant promise of new life to come. *Plus* there's the joy of seeing my sister again – how are you, Sandra? don't look so scared of me, I'm fine – and of being – thanks to her marriage to Tom here – can I call you Tom, Tommy? Or do you prefer Thomas? – I'm not sure he can hear me – anyway, of being, thanks to your marriage to Thomas, Tom, whatever, part now of this marvellous family. Because I am, yes, part now of this family, among whom – if that's not too formal of me – I number this lady Margaret – Peg, as I think you like to be known – yes: Doctor Peg and Terry here – happy Christmas, Terry – number these two human beings Terry and Peg among my most valued friends – and I am

* There is no crackling log fire.

perfectly sincere about that, even though I can see from your eyes – Terry – that you don't necessarily believe me – which is a shame.

Mum What is it you want, Robert?

Uncle Bob One moment, big sister, I'm still talking to Terry.

Debbie Grandad's not been well.

Uncle Bob I'm sorry to hear that, Debbie – but your grandad still needs to understand that when I say I value him as I friend, I mean it. Because I do mean it, Terry. I'm not someone who can say what they don't mean – understood?

Grandad makes gesture of friendly agreement.

Excellent. So – anyway – as I've said – there're a number of very persuasive reasons to stay here and make myself comfortable on the chair that young Deborah – are those real diamonds, sweetheart? – has got out for me – lovely: can I touch? –

She allows him to touch her ears.

Beautiful – really beautiful – yes really persuasive reasons to stay –

Debbie You're hurting me.

Uncle Bob What?

Debbie You're hurting me.

Uncle Bob I'm sorry – did that pinch? – I wish I could – yes really wish that I could but I can't. I want to but I can't. Did I hurt you? Sorry.

Granny What is it you're trying to say to us, Robert?

Uncle Bob Exactly, Peg – good question. Let me answer it.

Dad Is he staying or not?

Mum I don't know, Tom.

Uncle Bob Okay. Okay. It's like this.

We're on our way to the airport. Madeleine, I mean, and myself. We're leaving. We're leaving the country now. We won't be coming back. We've reached a decision and it's irreversible. Why? Don't ask. Don't even ask. We're going and that's that. You won't see us ever again. You won't see me, you won't see Madeleine. That's why she's asked me to come in now. Because basically this is the only opportunity she has – before we both leave – before we both irreversibly vanish – for her to tell you how much she hates you – yes hates you and abhors this family.

Now look – obviously – obviously I would much rather she told you this herself. I said to her: something like that, Madeleine, you've got to tell them yourself – not me. But Madeleine points out that she can't. And it's true: she quite honestly can't. There simply aren't the hours in the day. Her workload's appalling. And in fact she's doing her messages now – out there in the car – I know: on Christmas Day – unfair – incredible – but that's the kind of life she leads – now – do it – can't not – how can she not? – because once we're on that plane it's total dead time – hours of nothing – temazepam then nothing – total dead time till we land – and even then . . . even then . . . Well anyway – what was I saying? – oh yes, about Madeleine – about what she would like me to say to you.

Any chance of a glass of water?

And actually yes I think I will sit down for a moment.

Hazel brings him a glass of water.

Thank you, Hazel. Nice dress. Is it new? I like this – what d'you call this?

He takes the fabric of her short skirt between his fingers.

Hazel The hem?

Uncle Bob The hem – of course it is – lovely.

He toys with the hem of the dress while he drinks the water.

Grandad Ten years.

Uncle Bob What's that, Terry?

Grandad Ten years for a crime I didn't commit.

Uncle Bob I know. Horrible.
(*Softer and more intense.*) But look: this is not me speaking now, it's Madeleine. She hates you. She finds each one of you in your own way abhorrent. But it's deeper than that, it's deeper than that, it goes much deeper than that because it affects her physically – affects her skin – so even now – out there in the car – she's having to rub in cream. She abreacts. You're actually affecting – yes – fact – her ability to breathe. And it's you, Peg, it's you and Terry – okay, let's start there – because you're both so old, she hates you. Okay? She hates this   this   this smell you have – she says you both smell like flood-damaged carpet and wishes you were dead. Horrid. I know. And not just dead but wants to erase you. I wish I could select them – is what she in fact says – and click delete – I want – yes – to permanently delete not just them but each of their cells, each memory. What do I care about the little shops where they bought sweets, the old currencies they still think in? So what if Peg age five cut her knee skipping and still has the scar – and if Terry remembers the clatter of horse-drawn traps or the signalman shutting by hand the level-crossing gate, so fucking what, so fucking what, she says. This idea that an old person somehow distils

23

life's essence like a what? like an oil refinery? she totally
refutes. She totally refutes, Peg, *plus* there's the cost, there's
the unreasonable cost – Terry – of keeping somebody
like yourself alive. Why?   Why?   Why – says
Madeleine – are we bothering? And please: it's not me
saying this, it's her – yes, why do we bother with that
old fool? Look at his life – a succession of failures – one
business crashing after the other: tropical forestry – mail-
order cat-accessories – then there were the pre-booked
trips – am I right? – into space, for which you went on
taking the clients' money long after the whole doomed
project / had been scrapped.

Grandad Not all of them failed.

Debbie Leave him alone.

Uncle Bob Yes they did fail, Terry – all of them failed –
and please don't interrupt me, sweetheart, because I have
a plane to catch and what I am trying to say is long, is
very very long and difficult to remember – yes they did
fail. They did. And when poor Madeleine thinks about
that life of failure crowned now by your mental collapse
I am to tell you she doesn't just want to scream she
wants to drink acid.

Mum Robert?

Uncle Bob What? – (*Inward.*) But it's deeper than that,
it's deeper than that – wants to drink acid but it goes
much deeper than that –
    What?

Mum I think you should leave.

Uncle Bob You think I don't *want* to leave? You think
I get *pleasure* from having to stay here and repeat what
another person has instructed me to say? You think this
doesn't *hurt*? Because I'm afraid she's right, Sandra: this
is so typical of you – so typical of you and Tom in your

24

what? in your yes in your married bubble of stale air not to understand how your own brother could be suffering right now – yes? – yes? – look at me – yes?

I mean you've probably never seen the skin here, have you – Madeleine's skin – here – between her armpit and her breast – you've never seen it like I have, not felt with your own fingertips have you Tom the horrid rash she gets here when she considers your marriage. You've probably never run your hand like I have along the inside of her thigh have you Tom where hard lumps erupt between her legs when she considers your marriage.

It disgusts her, Tom. I'm sorry. I can't not say it. She insists I say it. It's the love. It's the long long terrifying years of love. I am instructed to tell you that those long years of love have burnt up – yes, this is right – have burnt up all the oxygen and what's left is a vacuum. They don't even hear my voice – she says – because there's no air left for it to travel through. House – job – school – kids – family – they don't even hear my voice – and their ready-made opinions switch on like the security lights protecting their property and illuminate the same blank space . . . (*He loses the thread.*) The same blank space . . . blank space . . . the same / blank space . . .

Dad You should calm down, Bobby boy. Have a drink – come on – it's Christmas / – relax.

Uncle Bob . . . illuminate the same blank space and yes – that's right – *if you will let me finish* – wants to take your head, Sandra, between her two hands and bang it against a wall – horrid, horrid – yes bang my own sister's head – fact – repeatedly against a wall until what she calls your   your   your   your *teeth* – yes – break in your mouth. Now – as for the two girls – hmm – as for the two girls . . . (*He loses the thread.*)

Debbie Uncle Bob?

25

Uncle Bob As for the two girls . . .

Hazel (*to Debbie*) This is all your / fault.

Uncle Bob As for the two girls . . .

Debbie (*to Hazel*) How is it mine / bitch?

Uncle Bob As for the two girls . . .

Debbie Uncle Bob – tell her it's not / my fault.

Uncle Bob As for the two – what?

Debbie Tell her this isn't / my fault.

Hazel Oh no nothing's ever your fault – little Miss 'I'm so pregnant / buy me a car'.

Uncle Bob As for the two girls . . . hmm . . .

Debbie I need to drive – tell her, Uncle Bob.

Uncle Bob What?

Debbie Tell her I need a car.

Uncle Bob What?

Debbie Tell Hazel I need to drive.

Granny Mums these days do need to drive a car, Robert – / Debbie's right.

Uncle Bob (*inward*) . . . but it's deeper than that, it's deeper than that, the whole thing / goes much deeper than that . . .

Grandad Not all of them failed, Peg – why did he say the space-rocket / thing failed?

Uncle Bob (*still more soft and intense*) Why were you ever born, Deborah?

Hazel Ha! – good question.

26

Uncle Bob She says: why were those two girls of theirs ever even born? – Horrid. – Wasn't there a test? she says. Why couldn't your sister screen them out? – Isn't that just the most horrible thing to say? – And when Madeleine thinks of your dividing and dividing cells glued to my sister's uterus, each with the same protein at its heart and now that same code of protein repeated and repeated inside young Debbie's mucus-plugged womb, she shakes me awake. Yes she shakes your poor Uncle Bob awake, girls, and bites right into me – can you imagine? And when I say bites I mean bites hard – draws blood. Then she passes her hand like this, girls, over my face – in the dark in bed, girls – like this – over your poor poor uncle's eyes and lips. And what she whispers is: that family – why were those girls of theirs ever even born? What're they supposed to find here on this earth? Trees? A cool stream? Do they really expect pear blossom to appear in spring? And now in wintertime – she says – when they have torn the wax strips from their legs in front of the crackling log fire – are they still expecting to hear the cheerful robin?

A long silence while he and the girls stare at each other. Finally:

Hazel Where does she bite you, Uncle Bob?

Mum Will somebody help me please with Grandad.

Uncle Bob (*reaching into pocket*) Ah – sorry – sorry – excuse me . . .

Two scenes develop at the same time: in the background, the family quietly and tenderly deal with Grandad, who has swallowed something the wrong way and started to cough. In the foreground, Uncle Bob answers his mobile phone while Hazel watches him.

Uncle Bob Yes hello?

Everything okay?

In the house – I'm still in the house.

I'm telling them now. It takes time, sweetheart.

I said it takes time – I'm not a machine.

I'm just saying I'm a human being not a machine: I can't can't – can't – whatever – I can't just –

I *know* when the plane leaves. I am fully aware of when the plane leaves, sweetheart – but we budgeted for that – don't you worry – the whole thing here is   is   is it's under control.

I'm sorry?

Why's that?

The *bathroom*? No. Listen to me: you can't –

You cannot come in here and use the bathroom, Madeleine. No.

(Shit. Fuck.)

Nothing – nothing – okay – whatever.

Love you too.

Mum That's it, Terry – just keep on coughing.

Dad What do we do, Mum – pat him on the back?

Granny You can try. Not too hard, though.

Dad Come on, Dad. Spit it out.

Granny Not too hard, Tom.

Mum Let's get him to stand up. Yes she's right: you're going to hurt him. Don't.

Debbie Come on, Grandad. We need you to stand up.

Granny If he's choking, he's choking – it won't make a difference standing him up.

Debbie (*getting him up*) That's it, Grandad. Cough it out. Are you better now? Maybe you want the bathroom?

Dad Would you like to use the bathroom, Dad? D'you want someone to wash your face?

> *Grandad starts to walk towards Uncle Bob.*

Debbie You're going the wrong way, Grandad.

Uncle Bob ends call to find Grandad coming towards him. During the following, the light fades.

Uncle Bob Alright there, Terry?

Grandad I like hearing a man speak – but that's quite some mouth you've got.

Uncle Bob Oh?

Grandad Yes quite some mouth. (*With increasing authority and vehemence.*) I didn't spend the best years of my life in prison just so you can come here now today with that mouth of yours and poison me – and poison this family.

Proteins? I have them in my urine – so what? I choke on a piece of meat – sure – does that make me stupid? I exported to China. I exported to Vietnam. Steel. Rice. I felled whole forests and I dined with ambassadors. I dealt in antiquities. I mined for cobalt. I wore hand-made leather-soled boots and I paid for the laces in *hard cash*.

Flood-damaged carpet? Go to hell, Bobby boy. You don't smell so squeaky clean yourself.

A noise. Everyone except Grandad turns to look. Madeleine has entered and tripped over something on the floor. She looks like an ordinary and unassuming woman and carries a big soft bag.

Madeleine Bit dark in here.
Lost a shoe. (*She pulls her shoe back on.*)
Okay if I use the bathroom?

Mum Of course, Madeleine. You know where it is.

Madeleine Thanks.

Mum Lovely to see you.

Madeleine goes off with the bag. Pause.

(*Faint laugh.*) When did it get so dark?

What time is it, Tommy?

Dad I'm sorry, my love?

Mum The time: what time is it?

Dad The time?

Granny He's not switched on. Are you switched on, Tom?

Debbie Daddy?

Dad What?

Debbie What time is it?

Dad He's dropped his pills.

Granny Five past six, Sandra.

Dad You've dropped your pills, Dad. Help him please, Debbie.

Debbie Which ones are which?

Dad I've no idea. Just help him, would you.

Debbie kneels on the floor and starts collecting Grandad's pills.

Mum D'you think we should put the lights on? Someone's going to hurt themselves.

Dad We've got the tree.

Mum The tree's not very bright, Tom. I think we should get the bulbs out. Please? Can we?

Dad Okay.

Mum and Dad open a cardboard box with light bulbs packed in newspaper. They put them in various light fittings and switch them on.

Granny Has Madeleine put on weight?

Bob Don't think so, Peg. Why?

Granny She looks bulkier than I remember her.

Hazel Bulkier?

Granny Quite fat, yes.

Bob Madeleine's lost weight, as a matter of fact.

Hazel Do I look bulky, Uncle Bob?

Bob Mmm?

Hazel Have I got bulky thighs?

Bob I couldn't possibly comment, sweetheart.

Hazel (*to Debbie*) What am I doing?

Granny You know quite well what you're doing.

Mum What time's your flight, Robert?

Bob (*to Mum*) Sorry?

Debbie goes on collecting Grandad's pills.

Mum (*laughs*) Don't be so rude, Peggy.

Dad (*to Deb*) Careful with those: they're for his memory.

Debbie What're the pink ones for?

Grandad Can't remember. Sorry.

Debbie Can you stop her doing that, Mum.

Debbie (*to Hazel*) Flirting. It's horrible.

Hazel (*to Debbie*) You can talk.

Mum I thought you were on your way to the airport.

Debbie Tell her to stop, Mum.

Bob Yes we are – we're on our way to the airport right now.

(*To Deb.*) I cannot control your sister.

General pause as Mum and Dad light more lamps.

Grandad (*genial*) What if it's stillborn, Debs?

Debbie Please don't say that, Grandad.

Dad Dad – just shut up now.

Grandad Keep your hair on. It's a legitimate question.

General pause as Mum and Dad light more lamps.

Mum Does Madeleine not have a family?

Bob What's that?

I said: does Madeleine not have –

Hazel She asked if Madeleine's got a family.

– exactly.

Debbie That's all of them, Grandad.

32

Dad (*to Mum*) Pass me another forty [*watt bulb*] would you.

Bob All of what?

(*To Bob.*) His pills.

Granny (*smiles*) Looking quite bright now.

General pause as Mum and Dad complete final lamps.

Mum You still haven't answered my question.

Fine. Just ignore me then.

Hazel Uncle Bob?

Bob What?

Hazel Mum asked you a question.

Grandad We had pears, didn't we Peg – *and* we had robins – we had a number of robins – we gave them all names and kept them in a shoebox.

Debbie Why did you keep / robins in a shoebox, Grandad?

Talking uninterruptedly from the moment she appears – and totally transformed – Madeleine comes back in. She has changed into a beautiful haute couture dress and radiates charm, charisma, conviction, power.

Madeleine I do   do   do   simply do not believe it! All these lights just for me? How wonderful! What wonderful lights! Tom! Thank you! Thank you! Oh – oh – oh – but the looks on your faces! Whatever has Robbie been telling you?! What've you *said* to them, Robbie? I hope you haven't been being indiscreet? Because this brother of yours, Sandra – and listen thank

33

you so much for letting me use your bathroom – can be horribly indiscreet. He cannot keep a single confidence to himself. *Plus* sexually too – well can you, Robbie?

Uncle Bob Where's the bag, sweetheart?

Madeleine Where's the bag? Where's the *bag*? I'm talking about your indiscretion, (*Takes his hand.*) I'm not talking about luggage – yes sexually he's all over the place, he's simply not continent – not that I care – it's his nature – I expect it – I encourage it – he needs the release – just you try stopping him! – isn't that right, girls? (*Approaching Hazel.*) I'll bet he's had this one already – did it hurt? – did he leave marks? – only takes him a couple of minutes – the bathroom? – or was it that sweet little bed with the heart-shaped pillow? – yes – yes – I can see it in her eyes – was it her first time, Robbie? – or can't you remember? – he never remembers, sweetheart – nothing to do with you – (*Approaching Debbie.*) And oh – oh – oh – oh – this must be the one who got pregnant – that's so sad – that is so pitiful and sad – but oh my God I suddenly realised where am I going to *change*?!
     Not in an airport toilet.
     No way in some shit-filled motorway service-station.
     Into a sheath like this? How?
     What d'you think, girls? Good fit?
     I can't tell you how warm and flexible it is – feels like I'm zipped into my own vagina. Pure silk. You can touch it if you like.

Mum Keep away from my children, Madeleine.

Madeleine Oh?

Mum Yes. Keep away. Keep away from my family.

Madeleine Keep away from your children? Why?

Mum Talk to her, Tom. *say* / something.

34

Madeleine I thought I was a friend. I thought I was a *friend* of your children, a *friend* of your family. But okay okay   okay –

      (*With new focus.*) Listen, Sandra, I realise I don't go deep. Neither of us goes deep like all of you. Do we, Robbie?

Uncle Bob I try. I have in fact been trying / here today.

Madeleine Robbie tries – but I don't even attempt it. Go deep? Why? No. And I will repeat that. No. Because this new life of ours – what will it be? Come on, Robbie – I said what will our new life be?

      Uncle Bob mumbles.

What?

      Uncle Bob mumbles.

What? SAY IT!

Uncle Bob Like a pane of glass.

Madeleine Thin – Tom – Sandra – girls – Terry – Peg – as a pane of glass. But of course he's told you all that. Haven't you.

Uncle Bob Yes, I've told them all that. Please – let's fetch the / bag now.

Madeleine Hard. Clear. Sharp. Clean.

      And if any one of you so much as *touches* it, you'll be cut right through – right through to the bone.

      They can keep the bag. Kiss, Robbie. (*Slight pause.*) I said kiss.

      Uncle Bob cautiously kisses her lips. Finding she accepts this, he attempts to make the kiss deeper and more sexual. Madeleine lets this progress, then tactfully pushes him back, and looks at the others in triumph.

And music!

She sings:

I don't need a woman to unzip my zip
or a man with a white arse cracking the whip
or some kind of what? fixed human relationship?

> Some people you lose
> Some people you keep:
> yes I'm a family friend
> but I don't go deep
> (no I never go deep)

I sit out in my car and I want to scream –
my skin erupts – I'm rubbing in cream –
oh why can't the world be hard, sharp and clean?

> Yes I'm often in pain
> there are days I weep
> like a nymph by a stream –
> but it doesn't go deep
> (no it never goes deep)

As a family friend it's my duty to say
I'm leaving you now – yes – I'm going away –
but if I was tempted to come back some day –

> went into the room
> where your kids were asleep
> and pushed pins in their eyes –
> then I wouldn't go deep
> (really – trust me – I never go deep)

But listen: I'm not some kind of inhuman thing –
you're not to imagine I don't want to sing
when pear-blossom garlands the pear-tree in spring

> that I've got no soul
> that my heart can't leap
> when the bud unfolds –
> just it doesn't go deep
> (no it never goes deep)

I've booked my ticket: I'm flying first class
to a cool place thin as a pane of glass
where I just have to swipe a security pass
to swim in the milk of thick white stars.

> It's a new kind of world
> and it doesn't come cheap
> and you'll only survive
> if you don't go deep
> (so I never
> no I never
> no I never go deep)

THE FIVE ESSENTIAL FREEDOMS
OF THE INDIVIDUAL

I

THE FREEDOM TO WRITE THE SCRIPT
OF MY OWN LIFE

2

THE FREEDOM TO SEPARATE MY LEGS
(IT'S NOTHING POLITICAL)

3

THE FREEDOM TO EXPERIENCE
HORRID TRAUMA

4

THE FREEDOM TO PUT IT
ALL BEHIND ME AND MOVE ON

5

THE FREEDOM TO LOOK GOOD
& LIVE FOR EVER

THE FREEDOM TO WRITE THE SCRIPT
OF MY OWN LIFE

— I write the script of my own life. I make myself
what I am. This is my unique face – and this is my
unique voice. Nobody – listen – speaks the way I
do now. Nobody looks like me and nobody – I said
listen – nobody can imitate this way of speaking.

— I am the one.

— I am the one.

— I am the one – yes – writing the script.

— I am the one – yes – writing the script of my own
life now.

Pause.

I said I am the one writing the script. Nobody looks
like me. Nobody speaks the way I do now. Nobody
can imitate this way of speaking.

— No way.

— No way can anyone speak like I do. I make myself
what I am: I'm free – okay? – to invent myself as I
go along.

— Yes I invent myself as I go along. I am the one who
makes me what I am.

— I said I am the one who makes me what I am –
okay? I've got my own voice: I don't repeat what
other people say.

— No way do I repeat what other people say. I am the one who writes the script.

— Yes I am the one writing the script of my own life now. It's me who makes me what I am – not Mum, not Dad.

— No way is it Mum or Dad making me what I am. No way do I repeat what other people say or follow – obviously – any kind of script.

— Fuck that.

— Fuck – obviously following any kind of script. I am in control – fact.

— I said it is a fact I am in control of my own life – I choose how I dress – I choose how to live.

— I dress how I dress – I live exactly how I live.

— I live how I choose to live *plus* do what I do.

— I do just what I do: I don't not do it.

— Yes please don't come here telling me I don't do what I do or do do what I don't. Don't you try telling me I don't live how I live. I am strong. I have choices. I can destroy Mum's toilet brush. I can destroy Dad's tools.

— I can build a space rocket in my own back garden – yes – *plus* – if I so choose – can destroy Dad's tools: the pin-hammer and the drill.

— Yes it's me who destroys Dad's high-speed electric drill, and it's me who destroys Mum's pink toilet brush. I destroy her sofa now she's lost her mind plus the two matching chairs. I destroy their TV. I take a sledgehammer and destroy their bed and the bedside lamp and bedside clock. I destroy Mum's bedside table and her dressing table with the three mirrors. With an axe – fact – I destroy the

42

wobbly chair. With an axe – fact – I destroy the
picture of two swans. I am the one who destroys
Mum's wardrobe. I am the one who destroys Dad's
wardrobe now he's dead and smashes the glass
ashtray. I smash the white plastic sun-lounger, I
smash the garden tools – the hoe – the rake. I
destroy the Saturday tea-trolley with the detachable
tray. It's me who destroys the pots and pans and
the electric mixer – yes the electric mixer and the
cupboard contents I mean all the plates bowls
knives forks spoons and packets of food like
macaroni. I destroy the old toys – the doll called
Sarah plus James Bond in his original James Bond
car. I take Dad's hearing aid and smash it *like this*!
between two bricks. It's okay: I can handle it.

— Yes.

— I write the script and I can handle it.

— Yes.

— It's up to me.

— Yes totally up to me – I write the script and I can
handle it.

— Don't you come here telling me I can't. Don't you
come here telling me I don't know how to live or
that I'm not desirable. Fuck off if you don't like the
way I speak.

— Fuck off if you don't like my religion, yes, or the
way I speak.

— Just so totally fuck off if you don't like my what?
what? what? – come on – say it – what? – my
disability?

— Racist.

— Anti-semite.

— Body fascist.

— Cunt.

— You terrorist – you body-fascist cunt.

— Fuck off if you don't like my heels or my short skirt. Don't you come here telling me how to dress: I have a unique style.

— I have a unique style.

— I have my own – yes – quite totally unique style: the heels – the skirt – or it may be a little hat.

— I may wear a little hat or I may cover my head entirely – it's my business how I cover my head and what I cover my head with. I am the one who writes the script.

— I'm writing the script right now – I'm choosing right here right now the course of my own life right now plus I am making sense of it.

— You think my life doesn't make sense? You think I've what? I've forgotten my own password?

— You seriously think I can't open the document of my own life? –

— *Wrong!*

— – can't change what I like? – can't delete whatever I like?

— *Wrong!*

— You seriously think I can't delete my own parents or alter the way I look? You seriously think I can't make changes to my own body and save them?

— *Wrong!*

— – or tell you when to fuck me or tell you when to stop? You seriously believe I can't access my

44

deepest love 24–7 and deepen it still more? You
think I don't have those skills? –

— *Wrong!*

— – can't write my own script? – can't turn a sex
crime to my advantage? – can't turn a chicken
sandwich or the scream of an abducted child to my
own personal advantage?

— *Wrong!*

— You think I don't know how to click on trauma
and drag it into the document of my own life? You
think I don't know where to insert the space rocket?

— *Wrong!*

— Yes – just so completely wrong, because I will insert
the space rocket right here. I have the will. I have
the voice. I have the style. I have the energy and
materials. Why should I wait? See me light the
twigs. Watch me ignite in my own back garden the
rocket-motor of damp leaves. Soon I'll be higher
than the garden swing, higher even than the roof of
my own house. Yes and all those sad engineers of
pure social misery who hate me to be weightless
can only watch through cardboard pinholes as my
own private rocket blasts towards Orion – mighty
hunter! – great X in the winter sea of stars! – and
moves magnificently into orbit. Let them try and
control me then! – let them attempt to impose
gravity! Watch me toss my piss-stained pyjamas
from ten miles up into their grey faces! See me step
out of my rocket wrapped in a bright suit of
aluminium cooking foil, and set off, lungs glowing
with pure oxygen, to track down the lost mass of
the universe!

*

45

Acceleration smears my face
as I go deeper into space
the earth gets smaller and recedes.
But not to worry: I don't care –
I've got clean sheets and nice clean underwear:
I've everything a human being needs.

It's not as if I'll be alone:
I've got the latest touch-screen telephone
plus all the different apps and leads –
and naturally Mum made me bring
Big Teddy and the garden swing –
yes everything a human being needs.

I write the script – key in the stars –
key in long rows of storage jars
in which I keep fresh human eggs and seeds.
What's wrong? Am I perverse
to fill my private universe
with everything a human being needs?

Check the controls – it's cold out there! –
no gas, no mass, no gravity or air –
zero is what each meter reads.
But not to worry – I shan't die –
I write the script and that is why
I've got a private oxygen supply –
lungs that inflate – a heart that bleeds –
Oh yes! I've everything a human being needs.

2
THE FREEDOM TO SEPARATE MY LEGS
(IT'S NOTHING POLITICAL)

—   I'm happy to separate my legs. I said I am happy to
    separate my legs – and when I say I'm happy to
    separate my legs, I mean it. I mean what I say.

—   I mean what I mean.

—   I mean what I say I mean: I mean I am happy to
    separate my legs – look.

—   It's not like I'm talking in code.

—   It's not one of those things where people are talking
    in code.

—   I don't talk in code. I don't say I'm happy to separate
    my legs so that people who've been educated in a
    certain way or have particular beliefs can sit here in
    this audience and think that I mean the opposite –
    no way.

—   No way do I mean the opposite.

—   It's not one of those horrible things where people
    all mean the opposite of what they say.

—   No way am I speaking in code – or trying to what?
    trying to represent something. I am what I am – not
    part of a group.

—   No way am I part of a group.

—   I don't join groups – I don't want trouble – I'm
    happy to separate my legs – look.

— I don't want to cause trouble at the airport: I raise my arms, I separate my legs, I let myself be searched. The longer I'm searched, the safer I feel. Plus I'm happy to queue: it's logical.

— I said: it's logical to queue.

— It's logical to queue, it's logical to pass through the arch of a metal-detector one at a time. It makes sense to go back if the alarm sounds, it makes sense to be searched and filmed. It's not like I'm looking for trouble.

— No I'm not looking for trouble at the airport. If the alarm sounds I separate my legs.

— I'm separating my legs. I'm letting my body be touched. It's a normal body, it doesn't represent anything. My body's okay. I've got an okay bum.

— This is my bum – it doesn't represent anything. My bum's not part of a group. My bum is happy to accept the way things are *plus* there is nothing hidden inside it.

— I've nothing hidden inside my anus. My vagina is empty. I let my vagina be searched. The deeper you reach into my vagina the safer we both feel – it's nothing political – there is nothing political about my body.

— There is nothing political about my body and there is nothing political about my holidays.

— Nothing at all.

— Nothing political at all.

— I said there's nothing political about my holidays at all – I come back refreshed – it's not like I've something to hide – I separate my legs.

— I separate my legs, I let myself be searched plus open my bag. I've nothing to hide – here are my things – holiday trousers, holiday hat. I'm not carrying an illegal cheese.

— No way am I carrying an illegal cheese or an illegal vegetable. These are my own children.

— Yes these are my own small children. I haven't stolen them, I'm not trafficking them. Their vaginas as you can see are empty and so are their cuddly toys.

— Oh sweet!

— There's nothing political about my children or my children's schools. My children as you can perfectly well see are one hundred per cent normal – raise their arms, separate their legs, produce their own documents –

— Produce – yes – their own tiny documents on demand, wait patiently while their toys are searched, and if God forbid I were to smack one round the head that poor poor child would be taken into immediate state protection. Because I admire the state. I said I admire the state. And when I say I admire the state it's not so that people who've been educated in a certain way can what? can smile sideways at their neighbour and think I believe the opposite. No: I admire the state. I admire its mechanisms for protecting my child just as I admire its systems for killing the unborn. It is proper to scan. It is proper to weed out the human material that could spoil my holiday, leaving me less refreshed.

— Oh excellent screening mechanisms! Oh scans of the whole human body!

— Scans of my holiday trousers! Oh probing radiographs of an illicit cheese!

— Deep scanning of the iris of my eye!

49

—   Cheese scans – deep scanning of my eyes plus click to explore my bank account plus click to identify my date of birth and current regime of drugs – I've nothing to hide.

—   I've nothing at all to hide: my medication's in this bag – see for yourself – it's not political.

—   My medication's in a transparent bag – it's not political – the deeper I medicate the safer we both feel – the deeper I medicate myself – the deeper I medicate my child.

—   The deeper I medicate my own child, the safer we both feel. I have a right to identify the molecule.

—   I have a right to scan my own child. I have a human right – yes – to identify the molecule that makes my child unhappy or stops my child concentrating or that makes him scream.

—   Oh look at my child run round the airport screaming!

—   Oh sweet!

—   If my child runs round the airport screaming, I give him the medication. If he coughs – if he fails to concentrate.

—   If my child says fuck to Immigration. If my child calls an air steward you cunt.

—   If my child says you cunt to a uniformed officer with a machine gun or begins to lash out with his fists, I medicate.

—   Oh sweet!

—   I pin my child down: I give him the pink syrup – I feed him the yellow capsule.

—   He loves to be pinned down – he loves the struggle to force open his jaws – and how calm –

50

—   – yes how calm he is now after the pink syrup –
how intelligent after the one-hundred-milligram
capsule – *plus* he's begun to read –

—   Oh sweet! – he's beginning to read!

—   – can pick out the names of chemicals and of
chemical manufacturers – can recognise the word
drowsiness, can spell the word discolouration. He
can even pop his own capsule through the gap in
his own teeth. He can even do sums!

—   I'm so proud of the way he does his sums – knows
there are a thousand milligrams in a gram and that
a thousand grams make up a kilo. He even knows
the per-kilo cost!

—   Yes my own small child knows the per-kilo cost of
his own medication. I'm so proud.

—   I'm so proud.

—   I'm so proud of my own child.

—   Yes so proud when he tots up the per-kilo cost and
he gets it right. Plus now when I read to him from
a proper grown-up story book how he goes shiny-
eyed! How he drinks in a delicious story full of life
and full of fully imagined characters so real they can
almost be touched! Watch him absorb the funny
and human things they say. See how he follows the
slippery antics of Susan and Bill – and of Susan's
best friend Jenny. Oh how deeply Bill loves Susan –
but how little he trusts her! He locks her away –
but even when she's locked away she lies – sneaks
out – goes back to her old friend Jenny – sprawls
on the soft divan and separates her legs. And Bill
finds out. Oh yes, the agony when Bill finds out
she's wet between the legs for Jenny! But instead of
confronting her, he only makes more promises and
gives her – Susan, I mean – ever more extravagant

gifts! A dress! A luxury motor car! Oh such is
jealousy! Such the complex self-lacerating agony of
human love! – but hey hey hey – it's not that I'm a
snob about this.

— No way am I a snob.

— No way.

— No way am I saying – what? – that there's one kind
of high-brow text-based entertainment for me and
my own small gifted and intelligent child and some
other kind of entertainment – some kind of – well
let me see – hmm – what? – some kind of screen-
based proletarian trash? – really? – is that what you
think? – for the less gifted? – for the what? for the
poor? Come on. You're joking. Don't give me that
shit.

— Don't you come here giving me that shit about rich
and poor – grow up – yes you heard what I said:
grow up – this is nothing to do with politics – this
is about me and how I feel.

— This is entirely about the way I feel.

— I feel what I feel: I can't not feel it.

— How can I not feel what I feel about my own child?
How can I not feel what I feel about my own
feelings? Because it's a fact that I feel what I feel
plus whatever I feel is a fact. Is a pure fact. Don't
you come here telling me it isn't. Don't you come
here telling me I should what? should resist security.
Why should I resist security? No. I need security.
I believe in security. I complete security. I zip up my
bag.

— I snap shut – look – my vagina – I proceed to the
gate.

*

There's nothing political about my children's schools –
there's nothing political about targeting certain molecules –
or about how I choose my holidays or hospitals:
DON'T GIVE ME THAT SHIT
JUST KEEP YR NOSE OUT OF IT!

There's nothing political about stories of child-abduction –
there's nothing political about my human right to
liposuction –
to the drug that I want or to the profits of drug-production:
DON'T GIVE ME THAT SHIT
JUST KEEP YR NOSE OUT OF IT!

There's nothing political about my holiday hat –
about how much I earn or who's feeding my cat –
there's nothing political about my right to be fat:
DON'T GIVE ME THAT SHIT
JUST KEEP YR NOSE OUT OF IT!

There's nothing political about replacing my heart
or about standing in line with my legs apart –
there's no place for politics in this or in any other work
of art:
DON'T GIVE ME THAT SHIT
JUST KEEP YR NOSE OUT OF IT!

Don't give me that crap about rich and poor –
stop droning on about what constitutes a just war –
don't you come here telling me what my life's supposed
to be for –
I said get that foot of yours out of my fucking door!
YOU'RE SO FULL OF SHIT!
YES YOU'RE SO FULL OF SHIT YOU CAN
KEEP YR NOSE OUT OF IT!!!

3
THE FREEDOM TO EXPERIENCE
HORRID TRAUMA

— Protect me. Terrorise me. Then protect me again.

— Protect me. Save me. Fuck me.

— Fuck me, scan me, then fuck me again. Satisfy me one hundred per cent.

— If I'm not one hundred per cent satisfied, return my money.

— Give me back my money and apologise.

— Terrorise me and apologise. Give me a new heart.

— Replace my heart with a new one. Repair my liver.

— Replace my heart and enlarge my breasts – enlarge my lips.

— Whiten my teeth plus fatten my lips. Make love to me.

— Separate my legs – make love to me – fuck me and abduct my child – surprise me on my birthday – surprise me with a kitten.

— Surprise me with dementia on my birthday, or with a lively kitten. Make me pregnant.

— Make me pregnant on my birthday. Make me pregnant age sixty-eight or still in a little dress age nine.

— Make me a nine-year-old father – scan me – bring me in for tests.

— Fuck and abduct my child plus bring me in for tests – test my blood – test my saliva – I have a right – swab my mouth.

— Take blood – scan my body – make scans of my brain – I have a right –

— I have a right to be scanned – I have a right to be offered a full range of serious diseases: terrible cancer, terrible suffering.

— I have a human right to terrible suffering *plus* to a horrid accident.

— Oh my horrid and entirely avoidable accident! Oh my worrying impotence!

— My failure to prolong intercourse.

— My failure to reach orgasm.

— My terrible fear of dementia – of childbirth – bad headaches – bad hangover – my reaction to shellfish – my anaphylactic shock.

— My shock – my reaction to fresh crab.

— My failing eyesight and stink of dental caries – my addiction to prescription drugs.

— My burning urethra, my chronic weight loss, my diminished responsibility, my stretch-marks, my broken nose and sex-addiction.

— My burning urethra, my chronic weight loss, my diminished responsibility, stretch-marks, broken nose and sex-addiction *plus* my addiction to morphine *plus* my addiction to shopping.

— My burning urethra, my chronic weight-loss, diminished responsibility, stretch-marks, broken nose and sex-addiction, addiction to morphine, addiction to shopping *plus* my post-traumatic stress *plus* my infertility *plus* my long long history of abuse.

— My trauma! My horrid abuse!

— My years of horrid abuse at the hands of those I trusted: my abusive mother, my abusive priest.

— My abusive father. My manipulative and abusive cat.

— My horrid abusive baby plus flashbacks of my abusive priest. Take blood.

— Take blood – scan my whole body – authenticate my abuse.

— Swab my mouth – authenticate my horrid trauma – offer me therapy.

— Offer me therapy – save me.

— Save me.

— Test me.

— Offer me counselling.

— Offer me a full range of anxieties.

— Protect me.

— Abduct me.

— Surprise me with therapy on my birthday. Fatten my lips.

— Traumatise me with a lively kitten. Whiten my brown teeth.

— Authenticate me – fuck me.

(*Softly.*) I said fuck me . . . go on [*continue*] . . . go on . . .

stop.

I said fuck me . . .

go on . . . stop.

I said fuck me . . . fuck me . . . go on . . .

— Remove and replace   go on . . .
   my heart.

                        yes go on . . .

                        go on . . .

                        . . .

                        . . .

                        stop.

4
THE FREEDOM TO PUT IT
ALL BEHIND ME AND MOVE ON

— Yes I decided I needed therapy. I decided I needed to change. There were things about my past I wasn't confronting. I needed to confront them and move on.

— For example –

— For example – yes – I'd never talked to anyone about my Mum. I'd never talked to anyone about my Mum and Dad. I'd never talked to anyone about my childhood.

— I had flashbacks –

— Yes I had flashbacks of my childhood plus I had problems with my sexual partner.

— I had problems I was not confronting: intimacy, for example – trust.

— I had problems with trust, I had problems with my body, I had problems with my partner's body. There were things about my body I wasn't confronting.

— I was angry.

— I was angry. I needed to put my anger behind me and move on.

— Yes I was angry about my partner's body. I couldn't talk. I couldn't talk to my partner about my anger. I couldn't talk to my partner about my Mum and Dad. I couldn't talk about the flashbacks. I needed to put my flashbacks behind me and move on.

— I needed to talk to Dad. But how could I talk to
Dad? I'd never talked to Dad. Dad never talked to
me.

— Dad never talked to me and Dad never talked to
Mum. Dad never talked. Did Dad have flashbacks?
If Dad had flashbacks he never talked about them
and if the phone rang Dad never answered it.

— Dad never answered the phone. The phone rang on
and on, Dad never answered it. Were there problems
Dad wasn't confronting? Things about his body? –
things about the telephone? Did Dad have flashbacks?
I couldn't talk to him.

— I could not talk to Dad. I could not talk to anyone
about my dad. I could not talk to anyone about my
mother's sister. I tried.

— I tried.

— I tried.

— I tried to talk about my mother's sister with my
partner but there were problems: there were
problems with my partner's body and there were
problems with my partner's cat. I was angry.

— I was angry with my partner's cat. I was angry with
my partner's body. I had flashbacks.

— I had flashbacks where I saw snow – could see
snow – could see a garden under snow – black
stalks of the currant bush – snow squeezed into my
woollen mitten – there's Dad by the space rocket
burning the pile of leaves, look – then it's gone.

— Snow falling from a grey sky into my face, look –
then it's gone.

— There's the smell of the damp mitten, there's Mum wheeling in the tea-trolley with the Saturday tea, look – then it's gone. There's that hard tapping on the glass – there, there, listen! – then it's gone. What did the flashbacks mean?

— What did the flashbacks mean? Why was I angry with my partner's cat? Why when my partner touched me did I flinch away? Was it the cat?

— Was it the cat or was it my mother's sister? Why was my mother's sister tapping at the window? Why did it make that sound? What was she tapping with – was it a key? I'd stopped enjoying food.

— I'd stopped enjoying food and I'd stopped enjoying sex. I'd stopped enjoying moderate violence.

— I'd stopped enjoying mushrooms. I needed to move on. I needed to change.

— Yes.

— I needed to think positively about my body.

— Yes.

— I needed to think positively about my sexual partner.

— Yes.

— And about my job.

— I hated my job.

— I really hated my job. Sorry. It's true. I hated it. I hated my boss. I hated her quiet way of standing behind me when I worked. The way she ate sandwiches angered me.

— The way she poked at the filling.

— The way she poked at the filling with her fingernail, the way she said Hmm not much chicken.

— The way my boss said Not much chicken angered me: I couldn't talk to her. I tried.

— I tried.

— I tried.

— I tried and tried to talk to her about my job, I tried to talk to her about my dad, about my flashbacks. I tried and tried to talk to her about enjoying sex but there was trauma: there was trauma in my boss's past. Why else would she poke a sandwich? Why else would she paint her fingernails bright green? My boss was damaged. Maybe her parents – who knows what? Was it about race? Was it about class? I refused to speculate.

— Was it about my boss's sexuality? I refused to speculate.

— Was it about the strip of light under her parents' bedroom door? Or under her own door? Or under some other door – the bathroom door? Was it about alcohol?

— Was it about misuse of alcohol or of prescription drugs? Was there a long long history for example of mental illness? I refused to speculate.

— I totally refused to speculate about my boss. I hated her, I couldn't talk to her, I couldn't talk to her about my job. I was trapped.

— I was trapped. I was boxed-in. I was hurt. I was fearful. I was angry. I was ashamed.

— I was hurt. I was silent. I was closed off. I was ugly.

— I was guilty. I was trapped.

— I was boxed in by my boss.

— I was ugly, I was fat.

— I was fat, I was too thin, I was too hurt.

— I was blocked, I was trapped, I was too ashamed.

— I was angry.

— I was angry.

— I was angry now my Dad was dead. How could I
talk to Dad now Dad was dead? How could I talk
to Dad about my flashbacks? Now I would never
talk to Dad about my boss's chicken or my
mother's sister's tapping. Now I would never talk to
Dad about Dad's body. Dad was dead.

— My Dad was dead and I would never talk to him.

— I would never talk to Dad about my Mum. I would
never talk to Dad about the lost mass of the
universe. I was alone. Yes I was alone. I hated
my feet.

— I hated – that's right – to see my own feet. I hated –
yes this is right – to see between my own legs now
Dad was dead. I flinched from my partner, flinched
from my partner's gaze. There were things about
my body I could not confront. I needed to put these
things behind me and move on. I wore socks.

— I wore socks. I covered my feet. I at all times
covered my feet and covered between my legs.
I was fearful, I was boxed-in by my partner's gaze.
I could not love, I could not love myself or trust my
partner. I could not separate my legs or trust my
partner with my love. I could not eat meat. I could

not eat sugar. I could not eat mushrooms. I could not eat wheat or dairy products. I could not look confidently between my partner's legs. I could not lie confidently across my partner's stomach.

— I could not eat nuts: there was no nut I could eat. I sicked up nuts.

— I sicked up meat. I sicked up fish now Dad was dead. I sicked up cheese. I sicked up marzipan.

— I picked through my own sick. I picked through my own sick while my sexual partner was asleep and ate it.

— I ate my own sick then sicked my sick up again over my socks. My socks were pink. My socks were dark blue. I wore thick orange socks. I couldn't sleep.

— I wore thick orange socks. I tried to watch sex.

— I wore thick orange socks. I tried to watch moderate sex. I tried to watch strong sex and frequent bloody violence. I couldn't sleep. I crawled into bed.

— I crawled into my bed and covered between my legs. I covered my head. My socks were pink. I couldn't sleep.

— I could taste sick. My partner slept. I could not trust my partner with my love. The room was dark. I covered my head. I covered between my legs. I saw Dad's currant bushes crowned with snow.

Long silence.

Oh help me – please – I need to confess:
I'm addicted to chocolate – shopping – I'm
    scared of sex –
trapped, hurt, angry – plus there's the stress of those
                    PANIC ATTACKS!
Hey   hey   hey – be calm – relax –
Just sing my little therapeutic song
then put it all behind you and move on.

Oh help me – please – I need to explain:
the abusive priest – the strip of light – the pain –
bitterness in my mouth – the wet piss stain and the
                    HORRID FLASHBACKS!
Hey   hey   hey – be calm – relax –
Just sing my little therapeutic song
then put it all behind you and move on.

Oh please please – help! – they say it's me
used my own child for child pornography
and that in point of fact it was my own family
                    I KILLED WITH AN AXE!!
Hey   hey   hey – calm down – relax –
Just sing my little therapeutic song
then put it all behind you and move on.

Oh help me – listen to me – please – please –
turns out I rounded up these Palestinian refugees –
shot all the young men against a wall
then the next day couldn't remember anything
    about it at all!
Not only that but when I clicked on the news
they were saying I'd massacred over six million
    Jews!
burned whole forests! – broke faith! – spat at
    the poor! –
trashed the planet! – started an endless illegal war
            PLUS I AVOIDED TAX!!!

Hey   hey   hey   hey – come on – calm down –
    relax –
Just sing my little therapeutic song –
we don't use words here like right and wrong –
say to yourself I deserve love I am strong –
then put it all behind you
        put it all behind you
just put it all behind you and move on.

THE FREEDOM TO LOOK GOOD
& LIVE FOR EVER

— I've moved on. I'm looking good. I look in the mirror: I like what I see.

— I'm looking good. I eat.

— I eat chocolate. I eat ice cream. I exercise. I look in the mirror: not bad!

— I eat a vegetable. It's a good vegetable. I eat a piece of meat.

— I eat meat, I eat a vegetable, I exercise, I look in the mirror, I like what I see.

— I eat, I look, I check.

— I check my weight.

— I check my look.

— I check my chocolate: yes my chocolate's still there.

— I check my vegetable, I'm checking my meat.

— I check my blood, I check my lung.

— I check for lumps.

— I eat, I look, I check my look, I meet my own eyes, I'm looking good.

— I'm checking for lumps: no lumps.

— I eat a fruit. I eat a chocolate. Oh yummy!

— I'm looking good. I'm looking pretty good. I said I'm looking pretty good – look at me.

— Yes.

— Look at me.

— Yes.

— Look at me.

— Yes.

— I'm looking pretty good. I'm looking pretty desirable. I'm working out. I look like a good fuck.

— I look like a good fuck. I look like I've got friends.

— I've got good friends. I'm checking my friends.

— I'm fucking my good friends then checking my weight. I eat fish.

— I eat fish. I eat fruit. I'm checking between my legs – checking my balls for lumps. I'm checking my hair for hair-loss plus checking my heart.

— I'm checking my skin for tell-tale signs. I'm checking my heart for lumps. I exercise: I can swim, I can run, I can stand on one leg.

— I can stand really well on one leg – fact.

— It's a fact I can eat fruit. It's a fact I can stand on one leg. Oh look at the fine fruit spray as I break the peel.

— Look at the fine spray: smell this fine orange. Look at me. I said look at me. Look at me eat fruit. Look at my mouth – not just the teeth – look past the teeth, look right past my tongue – look into my throat – come right into my throat and enter my stomach – enter my stomach, pass into my gut –

look round, yes, take a good look round my gut,
check it out, check out my nice long gut and
emerge from my arse. Look at me. Look at my arse.

— I check my weight. I check my arse. Look at my
arse. It's a pretty good arse!

— I'm bicycling.

— I'm bicycling a *lot*!

— I like to use my bike a *lot*! I check the distance
travelled. I check the time taken. I'm getting so fast
and fit! As each day goes by I shave off another
second and reward myself with a chocolate. I envy
you. I wish I could see my own arse from behind
the way you can see my arse from behind when
you're behind me. I wish I could see myself swim.

— I wish I could watch myself actually live – yes just
see myself being alive and continuing to be alive
and being perpetually alive and going on and on
and on like this living – not like in previous times
when people – remember? – stopped living and died
plus there was so much shit.

— Yes there was so much shit, wasn't there, in previous
times.

— There was so much shit about how badly things
were going – yawn yawn – about how people
stopped living and died. I mean I'd had it up to
here with how little fish there was – or how little
cash – with how children sickened, with how it was
all so bad and fucking difficult and yawn yawn
yawn – I just wanted to rock back in my chair and
scream.

— Everybody had bad haircuts.

— Everybody had really bad haircuts *plus* they were being rounded up and shot *or* their children sickened *or* there was an imminent I don't know what –

— Catastrophe.

— Catastrophe. A wave.

— Some catastrophic wave.

— Yes there was a wave or a dearth. There could be a blaze.

— The world was always ending, that's right, in a blaze of light or there could be a dearth. Time passed – oh yes – but time made nothing better – time made you feel like shit.

— Time made you feel like you'd wasted your life: either spent your life with the wrong person or never found the right person to spend it with – remember? – *or* spent your whole life with the right person but never of course realised until that person sickened and died and you were alone yes utterly alone and yawn yawn yawn – *then* came the wave, then came the whatever the annihilating blaze of light. There was so much complete shit, so much horrid emptiness: nobody swam, nobody biked, nobody ate fruit. I'd go into a shoe shop and there would be no shoes, or go into a theatre and there would be whatever –

— There would be no play.

— No play – whatever – what kind of fucking world was that?

— Yes I'd go into a food shop in previous times and find there would be no food, or into a bank and the

bank would be out of cash. I just wanted to rock
back in my chair and scream and scream. But *now* –

—   But *now* –

—   But *now* –

—   But *now* –

—   Yes but *now* –

—   Because *now* –

—   Yes but *now* –

—   Yes *now* –

—   Because what I am saying is that now when I go
into the fish shop there's fish – there is fish – mullet
and the red snapper – fresh crab.

—   There is – yes – mullet in the fish shop and ripe
plums at the fruiterer's *plus* if I want those rope-
soled boating loafers in the shoe shop then I'll buy
them. I will buy the loafers. I will boat in them.

—   I will boat – fact – in the rope-soled loafers – bob
on the ocean – dive from the varnished deck.

—   I jump from the deck – fact. Dive – swim – smash
up spray.

—   I smash up spray.

—   I like to smash up spray a *lot*! Look how I bob –
look how I float in the hot white light.

—   I float in the hot white sunlight near the boat a *lot*!
Then climb a rope. Then sip on a cold drink, bite
on a hot snack.

—   I climb on my hot friend on the boat. I bite on my
friend's lip. I'm snacking on fresh fish.

— I'm snacking on fish. I'm fucking my good friend.

— I'm biting. I'm biting my friend's mouth now. I sip on my friend's blood. I'm wetting my lips with blood plus snacking on fresh crab.

— I'm snacking on fresh crab a *lot*! I'm biting a *lot*! I'm biting down hard. I'm snacking on blood a *lot*! Look at my wet lips. Look at my stiff cock.

— I said my wet lips. I said my stiff cock.

— I said bright eyes, smooth skin. I said my slippery vagina.

— I said thick hair.

— I said flat belly and good fuck.

— I said my bike.

— I said I will live for ever – look at me.

— Yes.

— Look at me.

— Yes.

— I said I will live for ever – *look at me.*

Pause.

You're looking?

— Yes.

— Because my personal wealth and own privately acquired horizons are growing day by day – and day by day I am becoming more and more reasonable and more – yes you heard what I said – more so totally understanding of my own enormous capabilities that I can feel – yes can feel the time

coming when thanks to the indefinite extension of
my life I will be in a position to realise the potential
not just of my boat, not just of my bike and arse
and smiling eyes – not just of my sharp teeth – but
of the whole expanding spinning constellation of
my intelligence – don't you see? I said to you: don't
you see?

Pause.

I check my vegetable. I'm checking my blood for
lumps. I'm looking good.

*

My body's toned and you've probably seen
me running right past on my running machine
and my brain is alert and my bloodstream's clean –

> You won't see me die –
> it's not that kind of show –
> I cling on to life
> and I don't let go
> (no I never let go)

I'll always look good and I'll always have fun
plus I'll always have sex and repeatedly come
and I'll look in the mirror and always be young –

> With my sharp white teeth
> in a long clean row
> I bite into life
> and I don't let go
> (no I never let go)

I'm checking my chocolate – yes my chocolate's
    still there
plus I've got this new way now of doing my hair
so it kind've sticks up – look, like this – in the air –

which is kind've unique –
yes I think you should know
I've a right to life
and I'm not letting go
(no I never let go)

Yes I'm looking good – there's my hair – there's
    my eyes –
there's my firm round calves and scissoring thighs –
my expanding brain – it's incredible (just take
    a look at it) size –

plus a mouth full of crab –
but even so
I bite down hard
and I don't let go
(no I never let go)

Yes I'll always look good and I'll always be fun
and use my machine to run run run –
I'll have strong frequent sex and I'll violently come
till my blood streams hot and my mind turns
    numb –

Yes I'll set my teeth
in a long clean row
bite down hard
and never let go

(no I'll never
no I'll never
no I'll never let go)

IN THE REPUBLIC OF HAPPINESS

Tu non se' in terra, sì come tu credi

Paradiso, I, 91

*An enormous room. Daylight. Large windows suggest
a green landscape – but the landscape is indistinct.*
  *The room is completely empty – except, perhaps, for
what looks like an abandoned office-type desk.*
  Uncle Bob is alone. He listens.

Uncle Bob Maddy?
  Maddy?
  Madeleine?

  He listens.

Maddy?

  *Madeleine enters in the haute couture dress. She
smiles.*

Madeleine What?

Uncle Bob Where were you?

Madeleine I was having a sandwich.

Uncle Bob Was it nice?

Madeleine Yes. It was chicken. I enjoyed it.

Uncle Bob Where did you find it?

Madeleine Find it? I made it. I made it with chicken.

Uncle Bob Oh?

Madeleine Yes.

Uncle Bob Where did you find the chicken?

77

Madeleine Where did I find the chicken? Well it was in the sandwich. It was delicious. I enjoyed it. Would you like one?

Uncle Bob Would I . . .?

Madeleine Yes – like a sandwich.

Uncle Bob No.

Madeleine Are you sure?

Uncle Bob No.

Madeleine Not with chicken?

Uncle Bob No. Thank you.

Pause.

Madeleine So?

Uncle Bob So?

Madeleine Are you ready?

Uncle Bob Am I ready for what?

Madeleine How many times do I have to ask you?

Uncle Bob Have to ask me what?

Madeleine Robbie?

Uncle Bob What? Have to ask me what?

Pause.

Madeleine Is something the matter?

Uncle Bob Is it?

Madeleine No – I'm asking you.

Uncle Bob You're asking me what?

Madeleine You – you – is something the matter with you?

Uncle Bob (*with humour*) Like what? No. Bitch. Of course not.

Madeleine (*laughing*) Bitch?

Uncle Bob Mmm?

Madeleine (*laughing*) Did you just call me a bitch, Robbie?

Uncle Bob When?

Madeleine In this conversation.

Uncle Bob I can't remember.

Madeleine But you just said it.

Pause. He stares at her.

What is it you're staring at? Have I got crumbs?

Uncle Bob Mmm?

Madeleine Have I got crumbs round my mouth? Am I all smeared with chicken? Do I look sweet? I said: do I look sweet, Robbie?

She wipes her mouth with her fingers.

Well? What is it?

Uncle Bob (*smiling*) I have so much to remember.

Madeleine No you don't. What d'you mean? Remember what?

Uncle Bob The things you've said I'm to say.

Madeleine I haven't said to say anything.

Uncle Bob No. [*Not true.*]

Madeleine I haven't said you're to say anything: you can say what you like.

Uncle Bob No.

Madeleine Yes you can, Robbie – you know you can –
whatever you like. You can call me bitch, you can say
I look sweet, you can say just whatever you like. Go on.
Say it.
　What's wrong?

Uncle Bob (*lowers his eyes*) Help me.

Madeleine Is that what you're saying?

Uncle Bob Help me.

Madeleine Is that what you're actually saying or do you
mean help you to say something else?

Uncle Bob What?

Madeleine I said: is 'help me' what you're actually
saying or do / you mean –?

Uncle Bob I don't know. You said I could say anything.

Madeleine Provided it makes sense – it has to make
sense, Robbie – don't you see how important that is?
There have to be rules.

Uncle Bob Whose rules?

Madeleine Well my rules, of course – don't you see how
important that is?

　Pause. He reflects.

What?

Uncle Bob Don't leave me, Madeleine.

Madeleine (*faint laugh*) Leave you? Why would I leave
you?

Uncle Bob I know you.

Madeleine Oh?

Uncle Bob Yes I know what you're like.

Madeleine What am I like, Robbie?
I said what am I like?

Uncle Bob mumbles.

What?

Uncle Bob mumbles.

What did you say? Speak up.

Uncle Bob I said: I cannot remember what you're like.

Madeleine But I'm here, Robbie. I'm right here in front of you. You can *see* what I'm like. I'm like this.

Uncle Bob No.

Madeleine Yes I am, Robbie. Look at me. I said don't turn away like that *look at me.*

He looks.

Now. Tell me what I'm like – don't say you can't remember.

Uncle Bob Ah – ah – how beautiful you are.

Madeleine Beautiful – yes – and? Come on.

Uncle Bob Cruel? Are you cruel?

Madeleine Yes of course I'm cruel – but in what way?

Uncle Bob Mmm?

Madeleine In what way – Robbie – am I cruel? Is it I kill or is it I don't fuck?

Uncle Bob Mmm?

Madeleine I said is it I kill or is it I don't fuck?

Uncle Bob I don't know.

Madeleine Or both? Is it both? Tell me.

Uncle Bob I don't know. Kill who?

Madeleine Or is it my mind?

Uncle Bob Is it?

Madeleine Tell me about my mind – come on.

Uncle Bob I can't.

Madeleine Tell me.

Uncle Bob I don't know. Is it blank?

Madeleine Blank?

Uncle Bob Yes – empty – blank.

Madeleine Is my mind empty? Is that what you think?

Uncle Bob I don't know what to say to you!

Madeleine Her mind is blank – is that what you tell our citizens?

Uncle Bob What citizens?

Madeleine In your lectures – I'm talking about the lectures you give to our citizens, Robbie – I'm talking about your job – I'm talking about / the song.

Uncle Bob But why won't you let me sleep?

Madeleine I'm sorry?

Uncle Bob Why won't you let me sleep? – Why 're you always shaking me awake?

Madeleine Well I just want to see if you're happy.

Uncle Bob But you *know* how happy I am. You don't need to shake me awake.

Madeleine Oh?

Uncle Bob You don't need to bite me.

Madeleine I bite you to wake you up. I want you to see the tree. I want you to see the white flowers. And oh – oh – Robbie – the clean spring air! – and each blade of grass like a green razor! I need you to wake up for me and smile.

Uncle Bob Don't I smile in my sleep?

Madeleine No – never – you thrash – you grind your teeth – you thrash and you reach for between my legs.

Uncle Bob That's not true.

Madeleine Yes you reach for between my legs like you're not happy. Because have you forgotten?

Uncle Bob Forgotten what? I don't know.

Madeleine You see this is what frightens me.

Uncle Bob Forgotten what, Madeleine?

Madeleine I think you've forgotten how happy you really are. I think you're starting to forget how happy this world really makes you – grinding your teeth – grabbing – thrashing. Because what do you want? What have you not got?
Pause. Uncle Bob struggles to think.

Uncle Bob Listen, sweetheart –

Madeleine Oh?

Uncle Bob Yes listen to what I am going to say.

Madeleine Oh?

Uncle Bob Yes.

Madeleine And what are you going to say?

Uncle Bob Yes.

Madeleine I said what are you going to say?

Uncle Bob What?

Madeleine I said to you what are you / going to say?

Uncle Bob I don't know – I don't know till I've said it –
but listen – listen – you   you   you say to me
'the tree' – but I don't see it – plus you say to me 'oh the
white blossom' – but where – yes – where is the branch
that carries it? And when you say to me – say to me –
'clean spring air' why don't I feel it moving across my
face? Why do I only feel your hand? Or your sharp teeth.
    What lectures? Where are the citizens? Why aren't
they thronging the staircase? Or using small plastic cups
to drink coffee? Why can't I hear the small plastic cups
crackle? Is it I'm going deaf?
    You talk about the world but I listen and listen and I
still can't hear it. Where has the world gone? What is it
we've done? – did we select it and click? – mmm? Have
we deleted it by mistake? Because I look out of that
window and I don't know what I'm seeing just like I'm
opening my mouth now, sweetheart – look at it – look –
opening it now – here – my mouth – now – look at it –
and I don't know what's coming out – is this what I'm
saying or is this what you've said I'm to say? How do
I know? When will I ever remember? And of course
I'm happy but I feel like I'm one of those characters
Madeleine crossing a bridge and the bridge is collapsing
behind me slat by slat by slat but I'm still running on –
why? What's holding me up?

Madeleine Robbie?

Uncle Bob (*inward*) But it's deeper than that, it's deeper
than that, the whole thing goes much / deeper than that.

Madeleine Robbie?

Uncle Bob What?

Madeleine Pay attention.

Uncle Bob Pay attention to what?

Madeleine Please don't shout. Why is it you always get like this?

Uncle Bob I always get like this.

Madeleine Yes but why do you always get like this? What're our citizens going to think – mmm? Because you need to command their respect.

Uncle Bob I do command their respect.

Madeleine Because when you're standing in front of them and those hundreds of faces are lifted towards you and those hundreds and hundreds of gleaming eyes are locked – and they will be, Robbie – locked on to yours, and those – what? – what? – must be billions – must be so many billions of malleable human cells are being moulded, Robbie – yes moulded by me through you inside each skull by the sound of each thrilling syllable of our hundred-per-cent happy song – then you need to command their respect. I said: then you need to command their respect.

Uncle Bob I do command their respect, Madeleine.

Madeleine Then say it.

Uncle Bob I do command their respect.

Madeleine With each thrilling syllable.

Uncle Bob Yes. What?

Madeleine With each thrilling / syllable.

Uncle Bob With each thrilling syllable of our song.

Pause.

Madeleine (*smiles*) I can take you.

85

Uncle Bob Where?

Madeleine I can take you to see the tree.

Uncle Bob Yes?

Madeleine What would you like me to show you? the tree? or what? something else? shall I show you the stream? or what? the stars? or what?

Uncle Bob I do command their respect.

Madeleine Yes but I'm talking about something else now – about taking a trip.

Uncle Bob Yes.

Madeleine Am I not?

Uncle Bob Yes – to the stream.

Madeleine To the stream – to the tree – we could drive.

Uncle Bob We could go in a boat.

Madeleine We could drive – we could go in a nice boat.

Uncle Bob Could we fly?

Madeleine We can do whatever we like.

Uncle Bob We could go in a boat.

Madeleine If you like.

Uncle Bob We could go in a boat.

Madeleine Yes – if you like.

Uncle Bob We could go in a nice boat.

Madeleine Yes of course we could go in a nice boat but we'd need to smarten you up a bit first, wouldn't we. (*Smiles.*) Look at you.

Uncle Bob Oh?

Madeleine Yes: look at you.

She goes over to him and affectionately adjusts his clothes. It's the first time they've been physically close.

Why d'you always dress like this?

Uncle Bob I always dress like this.

Madeleine Yes but why?
And your eyes.

Uncle Bob And my eyes what?

Madeleine In the night.
When you shut them.
When you breathe.
When you thrash.
When you grab like that with your hand.
When I bite.
When I'm touching your face.
Don't you like me touching your face?
Kiss, Robbie.

Uncle Bob What?

Madeleine I said kiss.

*Very cautiously, he kisses her lips.
She smiles and is about to turn away when he grips her and kisses her much harder. She struggles to get free – a long and intense silent struggle – until he finally gets pushed away.*

No, Robbie – *stop* – what is wrong with you?

Pause. They recover their breath.

Uncle Bob Don't leave me, Madeleine.

Madeleine Why would I leave you?

Uncle Bob I know you. I know what you're like.

Madeleine Then you know I won't leave you.

Pause. She walks out.

Uncle Bob Maddy?
Madeleine?

He listens.

Madeleine?
(*Inward.*) But it's deeper than that, it's deeper than
that, it goes much deeper than that.

*Strange music becomes audible – a bright repetitive
phrase – half music, half machine.*
He listens.

Madeleine?

*Madeleine reappears with the source of the sound –
a small glittering box, which she places on the floor.
She hands Uncle Bob a microphone.*

Madeleine So. Are you ready?

He nods, and begins to mumble something.

Into the microphone.

Uncle Bob What?

Madeleine Into the microphone.

Pause. The music continues.
Uncle Bob speaks haltingly into the microphone.

Uncle Bob Here's our 100% happy song
it's got a few words
but it doesn't last long.

Hum   hum   hum
hum the happy song.

Pause. The music continues.

We make up the words as we go along
each word is right
nothing we sing is wrong.

Hum   hum   hum
hum the happy song.

Longer pause. The music continues.

Madeleine (*sotto voce*) We smile.

Uncle Bob What?

Madeleine (*sotto voce*) We smile when / it's white.

Uncle Bob
We smile when it's white, we smile
        when the pear-tree's green –
we're the happiest that human beings
have ever so far been.

Hum   hum   hum
hum the happy song.

Pause. The music continues.

The earth – plus Mum and Dad –
        the bedside lamp – the state –
have . . . have . . .

Madeleine (*sotto voce*) have burned to ash.

Uncle Bob
have burned to ash –
yes everything's just great.

Hum   hum   hum
hum the happy song.

Long pause.

*The music suddenly stops dead and all goes dark
apart from Uncle Bob's face.*

Madeleine (*sotto voce, from the dark*) Click on my smiling face.

Uncle Bob What?

Madeleine Click – click on my / smiling face.

Uncle Bob
Click on my smiling face and you can install
a version of this song
that has no words at all.

Madeleine Yes hum –

Uncle Bob
Yes hum   hum   hum –

Madeleine Oh hum hum hum hum hum –

Uncle Bob
Oh hum hum hum
the happy song.